Job and
Work Design

Advanced Topics in Organizational Behavior

The **Advanced Topics in Organizational Behavior** series examines current and emerging issues in the field of organizational behavior. Written by researchers who are widely acknowledged subject area experts, the books provide an authoritative, up-to-date review of the conceptual, research, and practical implications of the major issues in organizational behavior.

Job and Work Design

Organizing Work to Promote Well-Being and Effectiveness

Sharon Parker
Toby Wall

Advanced Topics in
Organizational Behavior ATOB

SAGE Publications
International Educational and Professional Publisher
Thousand Oaks London New Delhi

For information:

SAGE Publications, Inc.
2455 Teller Road
Thousand Oaks, California 91320
E-mail: order@sagepub.com

SAGE Publications Ltd.
6 Bonhill Street
London EC2A 4PU
United Kingdom

SAGE Publications India Pvt. Ltd.
M-32 Market
Greater Kailash I
New Delhi 110 048 India

Printed in the United States of America

Library of Congress Cataloging-in-Publication Data

Parker, Sharon.
    Job and work design: organizing work to promote well-being and effectiveness / by Sharon Parker and Toby Wall.
        p. cm. — (Advanced topics in organizational behavior)
    Includes bibliographical references and index.
    ISBN 0-7619-0419-0 (acid-free paper)
    ISBN 0-7619-0420-4 (pbk.: acid-free paper)
    1. Work design. I. Wall, Toby. II. Title. III. Series.
    T60.8 .P39 1998
    658.5'4—ddc21 \   98-8932

This book is printed on acid-free paper.

    99   00   01   02   03   10   9   8   7   6   5   4   3   2

Acquiring Editor:	Marquita Flemming
Editorial Assistant:	Frances Borghi
Production Editor:	Wendy Westgate
Editorial Assistant:	Denise Santoyo
Typesetter:	Rebecca Evans
Cover Designer:	Candice Harman

NWST
ALC0495

AKW9772

Contents

To our families

Introduction:
Setting the Scene

Recently, we were contacted by senior managers from a company that manufactures photographic film and paper. The company was making a multimillion-dollar investment in new computer-based technology to coat the "raw" film and paper with appropriate chemical solutions. Managers were confident that the new technology—by removing various manual tasks—would enhance the safety of the process and improve operational efficiency. Ultimately, they believed that the technology would give the company a clear competitive edge.

Although the managers recognized that jobs and roles would need to be reconfigured in some way, they were uncertain about how best to organize the work in support of the new technology. Some elements of the work, of course, would be determined by the nature of the product and the new technology. But these were relatively minor constraints on work organization. The managers appreciated that before them was a seemingly limitless range of options. This was reflected in the many questions that they had formulated to structure their thinking and on which to seek our opinion.

Those questions included:

- How should the remaining tasks involved be combined to form jobs?
- Should a strategy of specialization or of multiskilling be adopted?

- How much responsibility should operators be given for managing the new technology?
- Should the new work design be based on individual jobs or on teams?
- What impact would decisions made in each of these respects have on productivity, on the well-being of employees, or on their ability and willingness to accept future changes in technology or products?
- How should work redesign be implemented? What training would employees need, and what changes to human resource practices (e.g., payment schemes) and information systems would be needed, if any?
- Should the technology itself be reconfigured or altered to support the new work design?

The need to consider such questions about the design of work is not new. Collective enterprise entails a division of labor that raises questions about how to distribute tasks and responsibilities among employees, both whenever jobs are formed and whenever there is a change in the means or requirements of production, be this a consequence of technological, market, or social forces.

What is new, however, is that organizations are becoming more proactive in considering alternative forms of job design to those traditionally taken for granted. More and more companies are formulating lists of questions such as those above. This trend is reflected in a burgeoning of new popular terms, such as *empowerment, high-involvement working,* and *high-performance work teams,* that promote particular kinds of job designs. As Littler suggested in 1985, recent market changes have "forced many Western corporations to re-examine their philosophy of job design and control from a solid 'down to earth' perspective—that of profits" (p. 21). Job design is thus becoming an increasingly important topic, one that deserves fresh attention.

Our aim in this book is to document and evaluate research and practice on job design, addressing the sorts of questions listed above. Thus, we seek to map out the state of existing knowledge on how choices in the design of jobs affect attitudes and behavior at work. At the same time, we go beyond the present to ask what are the issues in job design for the future.

Six considerations characterize our approach. First, we place our primary emphasis on the design of jobs in industry. This is not to say that issues of job design do not arise in relation to office, managerial, professional, or other kinds of work. They clearly do, and we give examples of these. However, we focus mainly on industry because this is the context from which most contemporary ideas on job design have developed, about which we have most expertise, and in which we believe that there are particular challenges and opportunities for the future.

The second aspect of our approach is that we take an historical perspective. This is essential to understand job design properly. As Davis and Taylor (1972) observed, "The history of the origin of jobs has a powerful grip on the present, for this historical residue is the present conventional wisdom in the world of work" (p. 21). Thus, we consider the influence of historical factors on contemporary job design.

Third, we emphasize the essential link between research and practice. By its very nature, job design research takes much of its agenda from practice. Jobs are designed by people for people, and choices that are made for those designs, whether deliberate or unthinking, are the subject matter of research. So this is not an area in which research follows its own "pure" agenda remote from the "real world" but one in which applied issues are to the fore. This does not mean, however, that it is all one-way traffic, for research also contributes to practice.

Fourth, we adopt a principally psychological viewpoint. Job design has attracted the interest of social scientists from a wide range of disciplinary backgrounds, including sociology, labor process theory, industrial relations, and economics. We draw on these contributions. However, our main emphasis is on the literature of industrial and organizational psychology.

Fifth, consistent with the evolution of both practice and research in job design, our approach reflects a development from a relatively narrow conceptualization of the problem domain to a broader one. This is presaged by the title we have chosen for the book. We use the term *job design* to signify the narrower focus and *work design* to denote a broader perspective that links the job to its wider environment.

Finally, we take a critical look at existing research. We focus not only on what is known about job design but on what needs to be discovered. The latter need arises both because of inconclusive findings from current research and because of changes in work that give rise to new issues and variables to consider.

These six features are evident in the structure of the book. Thus, in the next two chapters, we trace the development of job design practice and research over three centuries. We start in Chapter 1 by documenting the early intellectual developments that arose during the Industrial Revolution and that were to shape job design practice to the present day. Our focus is on the simplification or deskilling of jobs, and we describe the early research to which that practice gave rise, as well as some of the early efforts to redesign work. In Chapter 2, we concentrate on a 30-year period, from around the mid-1950s to the mid-1980s, when research on job design was particularly vigorous and when the main theoretical approaches that remain relevant today were generated. We describe how these approaches led to two key practical developments, job enrichment and autonomous work groups.

In the following two chapters, we reflect more generally on job design research and theory. In Chapter 3, we critique the theory and research that provide the foundations of our current understanding of job design, pointing to a need for methodological improvements and a broader conceptual focus.

In Chapter 4, we present complementary approaches from the wider literature that inform job design research and help to broaden its theoretical focus.

We then focus on developments taking place within modern organizations and begin the move away from the narrow focus on job design to a broader notion of work design. Thus, in Chapter 5, we consider recent innovations in manufacturing technologies, techniques, and philosophies and how these affect work design research and practice. We argue that much as the Industrial Revolution determined the work design agenda of its day, so what has been called "the second industrial revolution" (Halton, 1985) calls for a new and expanded agenda. This theme is continued in Chapter 6, in which we look at wider trends in manufacturing and elsewhere, such as teleworking, downsizing, the development of a contingent workforce, and the changing composition of the workforce, that raise further issues for work design.

Because up to this point the focus of the book has been very much on the "what" and "why" of work design, in Chapters 7 and 8 we consider practical issues surrounding "how" to redesign work. Our aim in these chapters is to alert readers to some of the complex issues that need to be considered, rather than to prescribe the "one best way" (for which early approaches to job design have been so rightly criticized). In Chapter 7, we describe how the redesign of work has implications for wider organizational systems (such as human resource and information systems) as well as implications for multiple stakeholders (e.g., shop floor, supervisors, support staff, management, unions). In Chapter 8, we suggest some ways to manage effectively the process of work redesign, including the key stages involved in redesigning work, some useful tools and methods, and the critical role of a change agent.

In the last chapter, entitled "Conclusions," we present just that—some final thoughts that draw together our arguments in the book regarding the past and future of work design theory and practice.

1

Early Job Design Principles, Practice, and Research

As a lead up to the beginning of the new millennium, British television ran a documentary series called *People's Century*. The series reviewed the most socially significant developments of the 20th century. Among the topics selected (which included the rise of Hitler and the Second World War) was a program on Henry Ford and the assembly line. Entitled "On the Line," the program powerfully demonstrated how revolutionary Ford's working practices were at that time and how pervasive the ideas on which these were based have since become.

It was appropriate that Ford's development of the assembly line should have been included in the series, for it has been one of the most important forces shaping economic and social life. It is equally a key development in relation to research and practice on job design. Indeed, many accounts of job design take the assembly line, and other developments such as Frederick Winslow Taylor's ideas on "scientific management," as their starting point. In reality, however, the ideas that were to shape generations of job design practice and research have a longer history. Here we trace that extended line of development from the 18th century up to around the 1950s.

Early Intellectual Influences

The ideas that underpin contemporary approaches to job design can be traced back to views that emerged in Great Britain during the Industrial Revolution from 1760 to around the mid-1830s. The Industrial Revolution fundamentally altered the pattern of work within society. The manufacture of goods became an increasingly important part of economic activity. Moreover, whereas people had previously worked alone or in small community groups, the invention of large-scale machinery, and the associated development of factories, pulled them together in much larger numbers. This concentration of labor brought to the fore the question of how to organize and manage work.

Against this background, scholars began to consider the organizational basis of effective manufacture. Perhaps the most fundamental principle to be put forward was that of the "division of labor" as proposed by Adam Smith in his treatise *The Wealth of Nations,* published in 1776. This principle was that the making of a complex product should be broken down into a series of simpler tasks. Smith argued that efficiency was enhanced by such division of labor because it would lead,

> first, to the increase in dexterity in every particular workman; secondly, to the saving of time which is commonly lost in passing from one species of work to another; and, lastly, to the invention of a great number of machines which facilitate and abridge labour, and enable one man to do the work of many. (Quoted in Davis & Taylor, 1972, p. 25)

By the end of the Industrial Revolution, these ideas had been reinforced and extended. Thus, in the book *On the Economy of Machinery and Manufacturers* (the fourth edition of which was published in 1835), Charles Babbage, an engineer credited with the discovery of the computer, reiterated Smith's ideas and noted additional advantages of the division of labor, including that it meant the need for less skilled and therefore cheaper labor. He argued that

> the master manufacturer, by dividing the work to be executed into different processes, each requiring different degrees of skill or of force, can purchase the

precise quantity of both which is necessary for each process; whereas, if the whole work were executed by one workman, that person must possess sufficient skill to perform the most difficult, and sufficient strength to execute the most laborious of the operations into which the art is divided. (Babbage, 1835, pp. 189-190)

In short, in parallel with the technological advances of the Industrial Revolution, there emerged a social and economic philosophy of work organization that pointed toward breaking complex tasks down into a series of simpler tasks. Thus, development in mechanical engineering was accompanied by ideas for a particular form of social engineering in the workplace, each enabling the other. This was the beginning of what has become known as job simplification or deskilling—but only the beginning.

From Strategy to Tactics

It is difficult to gauge how much influence Smith's and Babbage's ideas exerted over practice during the latter half of the 19th century, or if indeed they were a reflection of practice rather than its cause. At the turn of the 20th century, however, developments in the United States associated with the work of Frederick Taylor and Henry Ford made these ideas highly influential.

According to Davis (1971), Taylor "rediscovered Babbage and created an approach called 'scientific management' " (p. 29). The exact historical link between Babbage's and Taylor's thinking remains a moot point, but there is no question that they are complementary. If Babbage can be described as having provided the strategy for job simplification, then Taylor supplied the tactics.

Essentially, Taylor proposed a method for determining the content of jobs. The question posed was: How can jobs be designed so as to make work more efficient? The answer involved using the reductionist disciplines of science to solve the problem: that is, to find alternative ways to carry out each aspect of the work, to determine which were the most effective, and to reconstitute the job on the basis of those "best ways." In his book *The Principles of Scientific Management,* published in 1911, Taylor (see extract in Davis & Taylor, 1972, pp. 29-30) suggested the following five-point plan for designing jobs:

First. Find, say, ten or fifteen different men (preferably in as many separate establishments and different parts of the country) who are especially skilful in doing the particular work to be analyzed.

Second. Study the exact series of elementary operations or motions which each of these men uses in doing the work which is being investigated, as well as the implements each man uses.

Third. Study with a stop-watch the time required to make each of these elementary movements and then select the quickest way of doing each element of the work.

Fourth. Eliminate all false movements, slow movements, and useless movements.

Fifth. After doing away with all unnecessary movements, collect into one series the quickest and best movements as well as the best implements.

In this way, Taylor added one key element to thinking of the time. Whereas the emphasis of Smith and Babbage was on the horizontal division of labor, on breaking work down into narrower sets of tasks, Taylor was concerned with the vertical division of labor, of removing from employees any discretion over how to carry out those tasks. Effectively, by specifying "not only what is to be done, but also how it is to be done and the exact time allowed for doing it" (see extract in Davis & Taylor, 1972, p. 28), this meant a separation of the "planning" of the work from the "doing." From this point, it was but a short step to suggest that employees should be paid according to their success in doing the task correctly and within the determined time limit.

It is relevant to note that the work of Gilbreth (1911), who exploited the then-new technology of cinematography to help analyze jobs, offered a more sophisticated method for job simplification than that proposed by Taylor. Effectively he added the "motion" to what became known as time-and-motion study.

The other major development around the turn of the 20th century, with which we began this chapter, was that of the moving assembly line. By 1914, in his factory at Highland Park in Michigan, Henry Ford had perfected the flow-line principle of assembly, in which, instead of having workers move between tasks, the flow of parts was achieved by conveyors, transporters, and other forms of machinery, and human assemblers could remain at their stations, with no need to move around the factory. As a result, the pace of work was controlled by the machinery, and ultimately management, rather than by employees themselves.

Thus, from the beginning of the Industrial Revolution until the start of the 20th century, one can see the emergence of a conscious process of job simplification. This movement began by limiting the number of tasks within jobs, developed to prescribe and standardize the ways of completing tasks, and finally sought to control the time that people spent on those tasks.

The Diffusion of Job Simplification

As Rose (1975) documented, Taylor's ideas created considerable controversy. An example of this was a strike against the introduction of scientific management at the Watertown Arsenal in 1911. This led to a call in the American House of Representatives for an investigation of the system, for which a Special House Committee convened in early 1912, with Taylor as a leading witness. The committee failed to completely condemn scientific management, concluding that it was a useful organizational tool, but also noted that it could give managers too much power. Paradoxically, the publicity during this period encouraged wider use of the approach. Similarly, Ford's lead in developing the assembly line was followed by other companies in the United States, both in the automobile industry and outside, and crossed the Atlantic to Europe. Again, though associated with resistance and industrial relations problems, the basic idea took hold. The more extreme manifestations, such as time-and-motion study, waxed and waned, but the core of Taylor's and Ford's thinking gradually became accepted as the norm.

The extent to which job simplification entered the orthodoxy within organizations is well illustrated by a study conducted by Davis, Canter, and Hoffman in 1955. They surveyed personnel concerned with organizing work in American industrial companies, asking them to rate different factors for their importance in job design. The single most important factor to emerge was "minimizing time required to perform operation," closely followed by "minimizing skill requirements" and "minimizing learning time or training times." The authors concluded that "the majority of companies believed in limiting the content of individual jobs as much as possible" (p. 7).

Studies two decades later suggested little change in emphasis, as well as an extension of simplification principles into administrative domains (Braverman, 1974; Hedberg & Mumford, 1975; Taylor, 1979). Today, similar conclusions have been drawn even in relation to modern manufacturing technologies and practices. For example, Ichiyo (1984, cited in Young, 1992) suggested that production strategies such as just-in-time can mean "the application of Taylorism by workers themselves" (p. 46).

Clearly, job simplification is not a universal phenomenon, and there is evidence that modern organizations are questioning its assumptions in a more fundamental way than they have hitherto—and changing their ways of working accordingly (see Chapters 5 and 6). Nevertheless, the thinking behind job simplification is firmly embedded in organizational culture and is essentially the default option. For these reasons, job simplification remains the reference point against which alternatives are compared.

Early Research

Although much of the practice of job simplification emerged from America, initial research on its psychological consequences came mainly from Great Britain. The Industrial Fatigue Research Board was set up in 1918, subsequently being renamed the Industrial Health Research Board. Shortly after, in 1921, the National Institute of Industrial Psychology was founded in London under the directorship of C. S. Myers. Both institutions took fatigue and boredom at work as their focus, responding equally to the questions arising from the long working hours demanded of civilians to sustain the military effort in the First World War and to the assumed consequences of job simplification. With regard to the nature of jobs, attention centered on the effects of the horizontal division of labor, as manifest in low-skill, paced, and repetitive work, rather than on the consequences of the vertical division of labor reflected in the lack of discretion over how to do the work.

A series of studies over a period of nearly three decades involved investigations of such jobs as bicycle chain assembly, soap wrapping, tobacco weighing, cartridge case assembly, and pharmaceutical product packing (Burnett, 1925; Wyatt, Fraser, & Stock, 1928; Wyatt & Ogden, 1924). The results confirmed the now-accepted view that repetitive work is dissatisfying and, if taken to extremes, is not necessarily more productive. The Industrial Health Research Board's Annual Report in 1931 concluded that "boredom has become increasingly prominent as a factor in the industrial life of the worker, and its effects are no less important than those of fatigue" (p. 30).

A later report brought a new dimension to the area. Written by Fraser (1947), this paper described the findings from a study of the association between job factors and the incidence of neurotic illness in a sample of over 3,000 employees in engineering companies. Neurosis (independently assessed by clinicians) was found to be most prevalent among those who found work boring; were engaged in assembly, bench inspection, and tool room work; and performed jobs requiring constant attention.

Returning once more back across the Atlantic, research in the United States took up the theme. Walker and Guest's (1952) classic study *Man on the Assembly Line,* conducted in the automobile industry, confirmed the relationship between simplified jobs and negative work attitudes. Similarly, Kornhauser's (1965) investigation of mental health in the same sector supported Fraser's earlier findings. With regard to people's mental health at work, he concluded that "by far the most influential attribute [of jobs] is the opportunity work offers—or fails to offer—for the use of workers' abilities and for associated feelings of interest, sense of accomplishment, personal growth and self-respect" (p. 363).

Taken together, this early research served to establish the importance of job design to psychological well-being. It confirmed the intuitively accepted view that simplified jobs were dissatisfying, and it introduced mental ill health as a potential consequence of exposure to such work. However, this early research was limited. It tended to ignore the question of productivity and performance, and it neglected to consider the effects of the vertical division of labor as reflected by a lack of autonomy in the job. Nevertheless, it did give rise to some recommendations for job redesign, which we now describe.

From Research to Practice

Job Rotation

The earliest suggested antidote to Taylorism and job simplification was job rotation, the productivity benefits of which were first demonstrated by the British Industrial Fatigue Research Board (Vernon, Wyatt, & Ogden, 1924). Basically, job rotation involves operators moving at regular intervals to perform different tasks, either on an obligatory or a voluntary basis. Benefits for the individual include reduced boredom and relief from repetitive movements, and a key benefit for the organization is the increased flexibility of the workforce (thus reducing disruptions due to, for example, absence). Nevertheless, because job rotation does not reduce specialization or change the content of jobs, it is probably most valuable to employees in cases in which fatigue from using the same muscles occurs.

Horizontal Job Enlargement

Horizontal job enlargement was the next suggested form of job redesign to gain attention. In particular, the British National Institute of Industrial Psychology played a large role in developing this concept in the 1930s when job enlargement offered a solution for a company producing wireless sets that was experiencing problems due to repetitive work (Harding, 1931).

As the name suggests, *horizontal job enlargement* refers to the horizontal expansion of jobs so that they include a greater number and range of activities. Typically, it involves combining two or more different simplified jobs to lengthen the work cycle and to increase variety. In some cases, it is possible to enlarge the set of tasks to such a degree that an employee completes a whole job from start to finish. Consider, for instance, an office environment in which each employee carries out a particular task (such as filing) for a range of clients. Reorganizing the work so that one employee carries out all of the key tasks (filing, mail, typing, etc.) for a particular client would be a good example of this type of work redesign.

Although the concept was developed much earlier, it was not until the 1940s and 1950s that horizontal job enlargement became popular. Walker (1950) carried out one of the best known early studies in the Endicott plant of the American company IBM in 1944. Enlarging the jobs of machine operators so that they also set up machines and inspected the quality of their work improved product quality, reduced scrap, decreased machine idle time, and reduced by 95% setup and inspection times. Many similar programs were reported within manufacturing settings in the 1950s (Buchanan, 1979). Phillips, for example, used such methods extensively to replace machine-paced assembly lines in their plants in Holland (Van Beck, 1964), Australia (Pauling, 1968), and Scotland (Thornley & Valentine, 1968). Typically, the approach was to create workstations where operations were grouped together to be performed by one person and where buffer stocks were introduced between the groups of operations.

Positive effects of horizontal job enlargement have been documented in many studies (Davis & Canter, 1956; Guest, 1957; Walker & Guest, 1952), although not all studies have reported positive outcomes (e.g., Nadler, 1963). One limitation of this type of redesign is that although it is particularly appropriate for reducing physical strain or mental boredom, its effects on motivation are always likely to be limited because it does not address the vertical specialization of jobs. To paraphrase Herzberg (1966), adding one Mickey Mouse job to another does not make any more than two Mickey Mouse jobs. Other types of job redesign, which we consider in the next chapter, differ in that they explicitly aim to return some of the "thinking and planning" aspects of work to the "doing."

2

The Heyday of Job Design Research, 1950 to 1980

T he 1950s to the latter part of the 1970s witnessed major theoretical developments in the field of job design. Two of these developments, the two-factor (or motivation-hygiene) theory (Herzberg, 1966; Herzberg, Mausner, & Snyderman, 1959) and the job characteristics model (Hackman & Oldham, 1976), were concerned with the design of individual jobs and came from the United States. The other, emanating from the more general and diffuse British sociotechnical systems tradition (e.g., Cherns, 1976, 1987; Emery & Trist, 1960; Rice, 1958; Trist & Bamforth, 1951), focused on group work design. Together, these developments not only shaped the research and practice of their time but, in the latter two cases, continue to exert an important influence.

The Two-Factor Theory

Herzberg's main proposition was that the determinants of job satisfaction were qualitatively different from those of job dissatisfaction. This idea stemmed from a review of the literature, the results of which were described in this way:

> The one dramatic finding that emerged was that there was a difference in the primacy of factors, depending upon whether the investigator was looking for things the worker liked about his job, or things he disliked. The concept that there were some factors that were "satisfiers" and others that were "dissatisfiers" was suggested by this finding. (Herzberg et al., 1959, p. 7)

In their initial study, Herzberg and colleagues interviewed a sample of engineers and accountants using a critical incidents methodology, asking them to recall times when they were particularly satisfied and dissatisfied at work and to describe the reasons for their feelings. From content analysis of the interviews, five factors stood out as determinants of job satisfaction: achievement, advancement, recognition, responsibility, and the nature of the work itself. Herzberg labeled these factors "motivators" and argued that they were intrinsic to the performance of work. In contrast, a different set of factors emerged as related to job dissatisfaction, including company policy and administration, supervision, interpersonal relations, and work conditions. These rarely appeared as causes of satisfaction. This second set Herzberg called "hygiene factors"; they were seen as extrinsic to the performance of work, being features of the work environment rather than the work itself.

The idea of separate determinants of satisfaction and dissatisfaction proved a powerful one, suggesting that what was necessary to keep people from being unhappy at work was not necessarily the same as that required to satisfy them. During the late 1960s, this theory generated more empirical research than any other in the field of job design and was highly influential among practitioners. From it, the concept of job enrichment first emerged, which consultants Paul and Robertson (1970) defined as "building into people's jobs, quite specifically, greater scope for personal achievement and recognition, more challenging and responsible work, and more opportunity for advancement and growth" (p. 17). We describe job enrichment more fully later in this chapter.

In retrospect, the validity of Herzberg's theory is questionable, and it is clear that something of a theoretical mountain was built out of a methodological molehill. The original cross-sectional study used a method relying on retrospective recall and on interviewees' own attributions of causality. The likelihood of bias was high using such methods, and causal attributions are not necessarily "real" causes. Moreover, the study involved a particular group of professional employees and it was a big leap to assume that findings would apply to other groups. Proponents of the two-factor theory also slipped readily from making predictions concerning the determinants of satisfaction and dissatisfaction to making predictions about motivation, performance, and mental health (e.g., Herzberg's 1968 article "One More Time: How Do You Motivate Your Workers?"). These extensions of the original idea largely preceded, rather than followed, the availability of supporting evidence.

Not surprisingly, as research findings emerged, the core proposition of the two-factor theory lost credibility. Support for the differential impact of various factors on satisfaction and dissatisfaction typically was found only when research was limited to the original method, and the occurrence of the expected pattern was shown to be related to social desirability (e.g., King, 1970; Wall & Stephenson, 1970). Given these and other disconfirming findings, it became clear that the theory did not stand up to the empirical test. Its initial popularity was no doubt a result of its simplicity, its intuitive appeal, and the fact that it filled an increasingly evident theoretical void. Paradoxically, however, the idea of job enrichment, to which it gave rise, was one that retained currency in the longer term; and Herzberg did manage to put on the job design agenda variables, such as recognition and responsibility, that the "scientific management" tradition (see Chapter 3) had caused to be ignored.

The Job Characteristics Model

The two-factor theory was superseded by Hackman and Oldham's job characteristics model, which has also has proved more enduring. By building on earlier work, especially that of Turner and Lawrence (1965) and Hackman and Lawler (1971), and by using additional research findings of their own, Hackman and Oldham (1975, 1976, 1980) identified five "core job characteristics" that relate to the motivation and satisfaction of employees:

1. *Skill variety* (SV): the degree to which the job requires different skills
2. *Task identity* (TI): the degree to which the job involves completing a whole, identifiable piece of work rather than simply a part
3. *Task significance* (TS): the extent to which the job has an impact on other people, inside or outside the organization

4. *Autonomy* (AU): the extent to which the job allows jobholders to exercise choice and discretion in their work

5. *Feedback from the job* (FB): the extent to which the job itself (as opposed to other people) provides jobholders with information on their performance

These core job characteristics were posited to produce "critical psychological states," with the first three (skill variety, task identity, and task significance) affecting the *experienced meaningfulness* of the work, the fourth (autonomy) influencing *experienced responsibility* for the work, and the last (feedback) relating to *knowledge of results* of work activities. Collectively, these critical psychological states were cast as determining four main outcomes—namely, work satisfaction, internal work motivation, work performance, and absenteeism and turnover. Moreover, the above effects, from core job characteristics to critical psychological states to outcomes, were said to be moderated by *growth-need strength,* or the importance that an individual attaches to challenge and personal development. The effects predicted by the model were held to apply more strongly to those with high growth need strength than to those with low growth-need strength. Figure 2.1 shows the most recent version of the job characteristics model.

Hackman and Oldham (1976) also suggested a way to combine the five core job characteristics to give a single index of the overall potential of a job to promote work motivation. This they called the "motivating potential score" (MPS), the proposed formula for which is as follows:

$$MPS = [(SV + TI + TS)/3] \times AU \times FB$$

The additive relationships for skill variety, task identity and task significance mean that more of one of these job characteristics can compensate for lack of another. The division by three signifies that all three together are only as important as each of the other two job characteristics alone: that is, autonomy and feedback. Moreover, as represented by the multiplicative function, the latter two are especially important in that if either has a value of zero, then the MPS is also zero. A job with no autonomy, for example, would have no motivating potential, irrespective of its level of feedback, skill variety, task identity, or task significance.

Since its original formulation, minor variants of the model have appeared. The specification of the core job characteristics and critical psychological states has remained unchanged, but modifications have been made with respect to the outcomes and moderator variables. In a recent description of the model (Oldham, 1996), shown in Figure 2.1, absenteeism and turnover are omitted from the

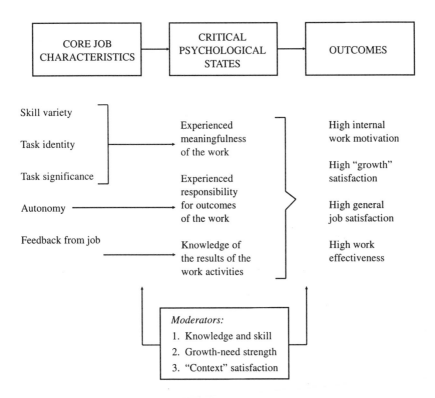

Figure 2.1. The Job Characteristics Model

SOURCE: From "Job Design," by G. R. Oldham, 1996, *International Review of Industrial and Organizational Psychology, 11.* Copyright John Wiley & Sons Limited. Reprinted with permission.

outcomes and replaced by growth satisfaction, and knowledge, skill, and satisfaction with the work context are included with growth-need strength as moderators. Such changes reflect findings in the associated research.

The job characteristics model has proved to be the most widely used theoretical approach to job design yet proposed. By drawing together much previous thinking on job design in a digestible form, and by developing a set of measures covering the key variables (the Job Diagnostic Survey; Hackman & Oldham, 1975), the authors provided an attractive research package and a set of user tools. Nevertheless, the model is not without problems. Research has revealed five key limitations (for reviews, see Fried & Ferris, 1987; Roberts & Glick, 1981; Wall & Martin, 1987).

The first difficulty concerns the distinctiveness of the five job characteristics. Many investigators have examined the extent to which skill variety, task identity, autonomy, task significance, and feedback are separable aspects of jobs or at least are perceived as such by job incumbents (e.g., Cordery & Sevastos, 1993; Dunham, Aldag, & Brief, 1977; Fried & Ferris, 1986; Idaszak & Drasgow, 1987; Schnake & Dumler, 1985). With some exceptions (e.g., Brass, 1979; Lee & Klein, 1982), studies have failed to reveal factor structures consistent with those theoretically specified.

Researchers have gone a step further to investigate reasons for these inconsistencies. Fried and Ferris (1986), for example, presented evidence to suggest that when respondents are younger, more educated, or in higher positions in the organization, they are better able to differentiate among job characteristics. Others have attributed the inconsistencies to method factors, notably the presence of positive and negatively worded items in the Job Diagnostic Survey (Harvey, Billings, & Nilan, 1985; Idaszak & Drasgow, 1987). In several studies, a revised Job Diagnostic Survey (with only positively worded items) has been shown to fit the a priori factor structure better than the original scales (e.g., Idaszak, Bottom, & Drasgow, 1988), though with no improvement in predicting outcomes such as job satisfaction (Cordery & Sevastos, 1993).

The second problem with the model concerns the role of the critical psychological states that are posited to mediate the link between job characteristics and outcomes. One aspect of this is that specific job characteristics have been found to relate to critical psychological states other than those specified: For example, feedback has been found to relate to experienced responsibility (Fried & Ferris, 1987; Johns, Xie, & Fang, 1992). The other and more general aspect is that the critical psychological states have been found to be unnecessary as the link to outcomes. That is to say, a model that excludes the critical psychological states and instead looks at the direct effects of the job characteristics on the outcomes fits the data equally well (e.g., Wall, Clegg, & Jackson, 1978).

The third difficulty with the job characteristics model concerns the proposed moderating effects of growth-need strength, context satisfactions, and knowledge and skill. In the original formulation of the model, Hackman and Oldham (1976, 1980) suggested that growth-need strength moderates the relationship between the job characteristics and the psychological states, as well as the relationship between the psychological states and outcomes. Most research, however, has simply tested the effects of moderators of the relationships between job characteristics and outcomes.

Moreover, although studies have generally shown that growth-need strength moderates the relationship between job characteristics and satisfaction (Loher, Noe, Moeller, & Fitzgerald, 1985; Spector, 1985), as well as the relationship between job characteristics and performance (Fried & Ferris, 1987), the same cannot be said for the other proposed moderators. No study of which we are aware has examined the moderating role of knowledge and skill. Studies of the moderating effect of context satisfactions have not consistently demonstrated the hypothesized effect; some have even shown the opposite of the predicted relationship, finding that people respond more positively to their job characteristics if they are *dissatisfied* with the context (e.g., Bottger & Chew, 1986; Champoux, 1981). The joint moderating effects of the three variables have also never been tested.

The fourth difficulty with the model is that there is little support for the efficacy of the particular form of the motivating potential score proposed. Investigators have compared associations between outcomes and the motivating potential score, which includes the specified multiplicative functions, with those achieved when employing a simple additive index (i.e., one that adds all the job characteristics together). Quite simply, the additive index has proved as strongly related to outcomes than the motivating potential score, if not more so (e.g., Evans & Ondrack, 1991; Fried & Ferris, 1987).

Finally, the job characteristics model fails to identify the relationships among the outcome variables and contains implications for these that are at odds with known evidence. Satisfaction, internal work motivation, performance, and (originally) absence and labor turnover are grouped together as outcomes. The relationships among them remain unclear. Because all these are posited to be the consequence of the same job characteristics (and critical psychological states), it follows that they should also be positively interrelated. That is, the circumstances that lead to satisfaction at work should also promote motivation and performance while reducing absence and turnover. Intuitively appealing as this may be, the implications of this aspect of the model are incompatible with previous research. Even at the time the theory was first proposed, it was already established that there was little consistent relationship between job satisfaction and either performance or absence (see Iaffaldano & Muchinsky, 1985, and Podsakoff & Williams, 1986, on this topic).

Given the above problems, it is clear that all the detailed predictions of the job characteristics model have not stood up to the empirical test. Nonetheless, this does not undermine its usefulness, because the main thrust of the model—that the specified job characteristics can be important determinants of the outcomes—has found support in both cross-sectional and longitudinal change studies. In general, much stronger effects have been demonstrated for attitudinal outcomes (job satisfaction and internal work motivation) than for behavioral ones (performance, absence) (see Fried & Ferris, 1987; Kelly, 1992; Kopelman, 1985); we shall comment on the significance of this later (see Chapter 3). On the whole, the job characteristics model clearly has some concurrent and predictive value, even though it is incorrect in its finer detail.

Theoretical interest in this model of work enrichment has continued more recently, albeit under the banner of "empowerment" (Conger & Kanungo, 1988; Spreitzer, 1995). A detailed characterization of this construct was put forward by Thomas and Velthouse (1990), who argued that empowered individuals have a sense of competence that they can perform the tasks, believe that the goals or tasks to be accomplished are meaningful, have choice over work tasks, and believe that their actions have an impact or make a difference. These dimensions have been empirically validated (Spreitzer, 1995), suggesting that they are indeed separable aspects of empowerment. Yet their overlap with the task characteristics in the job characteristics model is quite obvious: Meaningfulness taps into the concept of task identity, choice is synonymous with task control, and impact relates to the idea of task significance. Only the dimension of competence, or efficacy, is not explicitly included in the job characteristics model. We therefore strongly urge researchers investigating the concept of empowerment to draw on the existing and extensive body of job enrichment research. Likewise, those working from the perspective of the job characteristics model might consider to a greater extent than hitherto the concept of employee competence or efficacy (see Shea & Guzzo, 1987).

The Sociotechnical Systems Approach

The sociotechnical systems approach to the design of jobs originated at the Tavistock Institute of Human Relations in London during the 1950s (Emery & Trist, 1960; Rice, 1958; Trist & Bamforth, 1951). The approach stems from wider organization design theory developed at the institute. The core feature of this theory is the distinction between social and technical subsystems in organizations and the proposal that there should be joint optimization and parallel design of the two. It is difficult to attain a coherent and comprehensive account of sociotechnical systems theory from the earliest writing, but a paper by Cherns (1976, updated in 1987) did much to clarify its main propositions. These were articulated as a set of principles, which included the following:

- Design processes should be compatible with desired design outcomes (e.g., participative design for participative systems).
- Methods of working should be minimally specified.
- Variances in the work processes (e.g., breakdowns, changes in product requirements) should be handled at the source.
- Those who need resources should have access to and authority over them.
- Roles should be multifunctional and multiskilled.
- Redesign should be continuous, not a "once and for all" change.

The above is a general, normative, and largely content-free approach to organization design. When applied to the particular level of the design of jobs, however, it was supported by more detailed prescriptions. In contrast to the previously described approaches concerned with individual jobs, the focus was on group or team work. The key innovative proposal was for the development of autonomous work groups, which were considered to be the best way to optimize technical and social systems (Pasmore, 1988). In keeping with the principles listed above, the recommendation was that groups should be able to decide on their own methods of working (minimal specification) and should be responsible for handling as many as possible of the operational problems they encountered (variances to be handled at the source, enabled by multiskilling and access to and authority over resources). A wide range of terms is used to describe this form of work design, including semi-*autonomous work groups, self-managing teams* (e.g., Goodman, Devadas, & Griffith-Hughson, 1988), *flexible work groups* (Kelly, 1982), *high-performance work teams* (Buchanan, 1987), *self-directed work groups* (Wellins, Byham, & Wilson, 1991) and *self-designing* or *self-leading teams* (Manz, 1992).

From the point of view of the individual team member, six desirable work characteristics were identified—for example, that work should provide variety and that individuals should have an area of decision making they call their own (Cherns, 1976; Emery, 1959). The six criteria map closely on to those specified by the job characteristics model. For this reason, Hackman (1987) extended the job characteristics model to apply at the group level (see Chapter 4) and even argued that autonomous work groups have the potential to be more powerful than individual forms of job design because they can encompass larger and more complete pieces of work (Hackman, 1977).

Certainly, the sociotechnical systems approach has had a major impact on practice, as we describe shortly. Matching this practical interest, a considerable body of research has focused on the effects of autonomous work groups on people's attitudes and productivity (see, for reviews, Beekun, 1989; Cotton, 1993; Cummings, Molloy,

& Glen, 1977; Guzzo, Jette, & Katzell, 1985; Pasmore, Francis, Haldeman, & Shani, 1982; Pearce & Ravlin, 1987; Srivastva et al., 1975; Taylor, 1977; Walton, 1979). Research has suggested that autonomous work groups can enhance employee satisfaction (Trist, Susman, & Brown, 1977), reduce costs through group members' innovations (Walton, 1977), improve performance (Pasmore, 1978), decrease absenteeism and turnover (e.g., Walton, 1977), reduce accident rates (Goodman, 1979; Walton, 1977), enhance organizational commitment (Emery, 1959), increase perceived opportunities for skill use (Cordery, Sevastos, & Parker, 1992), and improve mental health (Herbst, 1974). Manz and Sims (1993), for instance, described how, by introducing autonomous work groups, a mutual fund improved customer service response time from over 7 minutes to 13 seconds; employees in a manufacturing plant reported higher job satisfaction than even white-collar employees; and a paper mill start-up project far exceeded its performance expectations. The potential benefits of autonomous forms of group working have thus been widely documented (see also Goodman et al., 1988; Wellins et al., 1991).

Unfortunately, many of the studies in this area have been unsystematic, with weak research designs. The few comparative or longitudinal studies that have been conducted have generally confirmed the positive effects of autonomous groups on job satisfaction (Cohen & Ledford, 1994; Cordery, Mueller, & Smith, 1991; Goodman, 1979; Kemp, Wall, Clegg, & Cordery, 1983; Wall & Clegg, 1981; Wall, Kemp, Jackson, & Clegg, 1986), although results are somewhat less consistent in relation to effects on mental health (see Sonnentag, 1996) and organizational commitment (see Cordery, 1996). Particularly inconsistent, however, are the results relating to performance benefits. For example, comparing three in-depth studies, Goodman et al. (1988) concluded that the greater the rigor of the research design, the more likely was the finding of modest or no productivity gains. Similarly, a meta-analysis (a statistical technique for combining the results of many studies) by Guzzo et al. (1985) of the effectiveness of 11 large-scale sociotechnical systems interventions (which included autonomous work groups) showed that their effect on productivity was moderated by research design (effects were weaker with more stringent controls), as well as organizational context (effects were greater in smaller organizations). On the other hand, on the basis of a meta-analysis of over 50 work innovation projects, Macy et al. (1986, cited in Goodman et al., 1988) concluded that self-managing groups had a positive impact on productivity, more so than other types of interventions. The contradictory results can be partly explained by the difficulty of designing rigorous studies to assess the effect of autonomous work groups on productivity (Goodman, Ravlin, & Schminke, 1987; Goodman et al.,

1988), but also by the possibility that this form of work redesign promotes performance benefits in some circumstances but not in others (see Chapter 3, the section "A Need to Consider Contingencies").

Apart from the above problems associated with examining the effects of work redesign on performance (considered in the next chapter, in which we critique job design research more broadly), several criticisms have been specifically aimed at the sociotechnical systems approach. In particular, the approach offers only general and vague guidance on the nature of job design and the expected consequences for outcomes. For example, it offers no guidance on which aspects of work will promote the strongest outcomes. As Cherns and Davis (1975) stated, the sociotechnical systems approach requires the use of a number of nonexistent dictionaries to be put into practice. Without a clearer agreed-on framework to identify the key features of work and their particular effects, one that integrates the many different aspects of the approach, it is difficult to relate empirical evidence with "theory" and thus to form judgments about the validity of the latter.

Other more specific criticisms of the sociotechnical systems approach are that it has focused excessively on mass production contexts, tends to see autonomous work groups as the "standard solution," and pays little attention to organizational culture or individual differences (Kompier, 1996).

Despite these problems, however, there can be no denying that this approach to work design has proved to be of value. It has spurred the development of other models of group work design that offer more precise guidance (see Chapter 4, the section "Models of Group Effectiveness"). Moreover, if the job characteristics model is claimed to have had the greatest impact on job design research, then the sociotechnical systems approach, and its derivative notion of autonomous work groups, can be argued to have had the stronger influence over practice. To the practice we now turn.

From Theory to Practice

The three approaches described above have given rise to practical suggestions about how jobs should be designed. In clear contrast to job rotation or horizontal job enlargement (described in the previous chapter), the emphasis of these job design suggestions is on enhancing the discretion or autonomy that people can exercise in carrying out their work, thus reversing the vertical division of labor that Taylor sought to achieve. For both the two-factor theory and the job characteristics model, this idea has been called *job enrichment,* whereas from the sociotechnical systems approach, the practical suggestion has been that of autonomous work groups. We describe these work design interventions in more detail now, with an example of each to make them more explicit. Later, in Chapters 7 and 8, we highlight some of the practical difficulties associated with restructuring work and point to some of the broader organizational changes that will be necessary for work redesign to be effective.

Job Enrichment

Job enrichment (also referred to by Kelly, 1982, as "vertical role integration") can be of two broad forms. The first involves increasing employee responsibility for those decisions traditionally made by a supervisor, such as decisions about scheduling of work and the allocation of tasks. The second involves upgrading jobs to include extra skilled tasks that are not necessarily elements of supervisory work (e.g., production employees undertake basic maintenance or diagnostic work, or office staff perform more skilled tasks, such as ordering supplies). In terms of the actual process of work redesign, various principles, or "design criteria," can be used to enrich work. Recommendations from a range of sources (e.g., Aldag & Brief, 1979; Birchall, 1975; Herzberg, 1968) include the following:

- Arrange work in a way that allows the individual employee to influence his or her own working situation, work methods, and pace. Devise methods to eliminate or minimize pacing.
- Where possible, combine interdependent tasks into a job.
- Aim to group tasks into a meaningful job that allows for an overview and understanding of the work process as a whole. Employees should be able to perceive the end product or service as contributing to some part of the organization's objectives.
- Provide a sufficient variety of tasks within the job, and include tasks that offer some degree of employee responsibility and make use of the skills and knowledge valued by the individual.
- Arrange work in a way that makes it possible for the individual employee to satisfy time claims from roles and obligations outside work (e.g., family commitments).
- Provide opportunities for an employee to achieve outcomes that he or she perceives as desirable (e.g., personal advancement in the form of increased salary, scope for development of expertise, improved status within a work group, and a more challenging job).
- Ensure that employees get feedback on their performance, ideally from the task as well as from the supervisor. Provide internal and external customer feedback directly to employees.
- Provide employees with the information they need to make decisions.

BOX 2.1. Job Enrichment for Airline Reservation Clerks

Before job enrichment, the job of 16 airline reservation clerks involved answering client queries, quoting fares from a manual, checking and inputting reservations into a computer, and making any special arrangements (concerning diet, etc.). On occasion, they had to telephone clients to address more complex queries.

After training in job design principles, supervisors (assisted by specialists) held brainstorming sessions to devise ways to improve the clerks' jobs. The ideas were evaluated by group members, and the following changes resulted:

- Clerks were given authority to deal with some special requests formerly referred to supervisors.
- Clerks arranged their own work rota to meet staffing requirements.
- Clerks were given authority and encouraged to quote complex fares, formerly the responsibility of a specialist department.
- Clerks were encouraged to pass on useful information to the marketing department.
- Clerks were consulted regarding periodic modifications to computerized reservation systems.
- Each clerk was given responsibility for maintaining tariff manuals and a personal file of travel information.

Outcomes of the job enrichment included an increase in efficiency and an increase in employee morale.

SOURCE: Gormon and Molloy (1972, cited in Birchall, 1975).

Box 2.1 describes an example of job enrichment for airline reservation clerks (see Birchall, 1975, for further examples in a range of different industries).

Autonomous Work Groups

The introduction of autonomous work groups involves redesigning work at the group level, and this is the major way in which it can be differentiated from job enrichment. Essentially, the defining feature of autonomous group working is that employees have discretion over day-to-day operational decisions (i.e., relating to who does what, when, and how) as well as input into the running of the group (e.g., training team members and selecting new members). Typically, the tasks within the group are interdependent and together make a whole product or service. In modern manufacturing settings, for example, autonomous work groups are often introduced in conjunction with product-based cells (see Chapter 5, the section

"Cellular Manufacturing"). Team members usually have a variety of skills consistent with the need to perform a range of tasks, and the team receives regular performance feedback (Wall et al., 1986).

Design principles for autonomous work groups, based on sociotechnical systems theory, include the following:

- Group interdependent tasks to make a meaningful set and to involve a balance between less popular and desirable tasks.
- Provide clear performance criteria for the team as a whole.
- Provide clear feedback on group performance.
- As far as possible, leave methods of working to employee discretion (i.e., minimal specification).
- Allow employees to control variances at the source, but ensure that they have the necessary knowledge, skills, and information to intervene.
- Allow the group to control equipment, materials, and other resources, making them responsible for their prudent use.
- Increase the skill level of employees to allow flexible responses to uncertainties (but note that complete multiskilling might result in redundancy of skills).
- Ensure that selection, training, payment systems, and so forth are congruent with the work design (see Chapter 7 for more on this point).
- Regularly review and evaluate the work design.

Well-publicized and early applications of autonomous work groups include those by Volvo (see, for an analysis, Pontusson, 1990), Topeka (Walton, 1972), and General Foods (Walton, 1977, 1982). More recent applications include those by Levi Strauss, AT&T, and Xerox (Appelbaum & Batt, 1994), and examples have been reported in a range of other contexts, such as in the chemical industry, the electronics industry (Buchanan & McCalman, 1989; Parker & Jackson, 1994), and the motor vehicles industry (Parker & Slaughter, 1988). Box 2.2 describes an example of the introduction of autonomous work groups within a sweets factory.

It is important to observe that autonomous work groups do not always come in the same format. One way in which groups vary is in how they are supervised, ranging from the situation in which where there is no immediate supervisor to the situation in which there is a team leader position that might or might not be rotated among team members (Dunphy & Bryant, 1996; see Chapter 7). Another way in which groups vary is in the degree of intragroup task specialization (multiskilling). Cordery (1996) suggested that autonomous work groups tend to be characterized by medium to high degrees of *vertical multiskilling* (i.e., learning elements of the supervisory role); medium to high degrees of *horizontal multiskilling* (i.e., learning tasks from traditionally separate occupational or job families, as in the case of a

BOX 2.2. Autonomous Work Groups in a Sweet Factory

To improve their performance, a sweets manufacturer implemented autonomous work groups within production. Before the work redesign, employees typically worked within a specific part of the process, carrying out a limited task. However, following the introduction of autonomous work groups, employees worked in groups of 8 to 12 people and were expected to carry out several of the types of tasks involved in the production process. Group members were collectively responsible for running the group and reaching production targets. They were also involved in new activities, such as quality inspection, solving local problems, and analyzing performance data. The groups had no supervisor but reported directly to a manager responsible for three or more other groups. The contrast between this and the traditional way of working within the company is illustrated by Table 1.

TABLE 1

The Properties of Traditional Work Design and
Autonomous Work Groups in the Case of a Sweets Factory

Task/Role	Traditional	Autonomous Work Groups
Wrapping sweets	Operators	Operators
Packing sweets	Operators	Operators
Cleaning/hygiene	Operators	Operators
Quality	Inspectors	Operators
Routine maintenance	Inspectors	Operators
Ordering raw materials	Supervisor	Operators
Delivering finished goods	Supervisor	Operators
Record keeping	Supervisor	Operators
Calling for engineers	Supervisor	Operators
Job allocation	Supervisor	Operators
Arranging breaks	Supervisor	Operators
Training recruits	Trainers	Operators
Selection	Supervisor/personnel	Operators/personnel
Discipline	Supervisor/manager	Manager
Policy implication	Manager	Manager
Ratio of operators to immediate supervisor	12:1	45:1

The job redesign was carefully evaluated using a longitudinal research design and multiple comparison groups. Results showed clear benefits for employee satisfaction but no demonstrable effect on mental health. The volume of sweets produced by autonomous work groups was equivalent to that under the traditional form of working, but productivity was higher because of lower indirect (i.e., supervisory) costs. The authors concluded that work group autonomy had specific rather than universal effects on employee attitudes and behavior.

SOURCE: Reported by Wall, Kemp, Jackson, and Clegg (1986).

mine operator learning to drive a truck and carry out laboratory tasks); and low levels of *depth multiskilling* (i.e., developing skills that are within the same occupational or skill group but that usually have a different job title, as in the case of a mechanical tradesperson learning advanced hydraulics).

Groups can also vary in the extent to which members control all of the relevant support tasks, such as quality and maintenance, as well as the degree to which they manage their own design (Goodman et al., 1988). Regarding the latter aspect, "self-designing" teams (Hackman, 1987) or "self-leading" teams (Manz, 1992) have control over the design of the team itself. Thus, group members have influence over the strategic decisions of "what" the group does and "why," rather than just over "how" (e.g., they have direct involvement in deciding the group's purpose and have the right to choose external group leaders). Manz (1992) argued that self-leading teams are especially appropriate in contexts with ambiguous and changeable tasks.

Autonomous work groups, in all their forms and sizes, are increasingly popular. Lawler, Mohrman, and Ledford (1992) reported that the use of self-managing teams increased from 28% in 1990 to 47% in 1992, and Osterman (1994) showed that the growth of this practice exceeds other workplace innovations such as quality circles and total quality management. This pattern appears to be set to continue. Goodman et al. (1988, p. 324) predicted that with the cultural trend toward participation and the widespread use of new flexible technologies, autonomous work groups will become even more popular and will spread into broader domains, such as service and support settings and managerial levels. For the many companies who have experimented with less complex forms of groups (such as quality circles), Goodman et al. anticipated that autonomous work groups will be their next challenging step.

3

A Critique of Existing Theory and Research

Thus far, we have described the most influential job design theories (i.e., Herzberg's two-factor theory, the job characteristics model, and the socio-technical systems approach)[1] and some of the key problems specific to these. Here we take a more critical perspective, charting some limitations that beset the general field of job design research. Our critique remains "within tradition": That is, although we argue that further development of the field is inhibited by methodological weaknesses and a narrow focus, we accept as valid the core ideas of the job characteristics approach. Our objective is straightforward: to draw attention to the main ways in which the field as it stands might develop.

Methodological Issues

Emphasis on Perceptual Measures of Job Characteristics

Job design research has typically proceeded by using perceptual measures of job characteristics. That is to say, much of the research has used respondents' ratings of their own job properties to describe their work rather than objective or independent ratings. From a theoretical perspective, the use of self-ratings makes sense. It is the personal meaning of a job that is expected to influence well-being, and another person's rating of the job is not necessarily valid or appropriate (Warr, in press). Nevertheless, the use of self-ratings, especially within a cross-sectional framework, has led to concern about the validity of the findings (Roberts & Glick, 1981).

One concern is that social and situational factors, such as colleagues' attitudes, might influence people's perceptions of and feelings about their jobs more than the objective characteristics of the job per se (e.g., Algera, 1983). A further concern is that arising from "common-method variance." That is, there is a greater likelihood of high correlations among job content and outcome variables when all variables are measured using similar measurement formats (e.g., self-report items in a single questionnaire) than when different measurement methods are used. For example, respondents who have a happy disposition are likely to rate their job features positively and to rate their job satisfaction as high, even though there is no causal association between these two aspects.

Despite these concerns, reviews of the literature generally conclude that the job characteristics approach cannot be dismissed solely as an artifact of the use of perceptual measures of job features (e.g., Wall & Martin, 1987). Considering the degree to which employee self-ratings map onto objective job features, Oldham (1996) recently summarized three streams of relevant research. The first set of studies concern the convergence between self-ratings and ratings from external observers, such as peers or researchers (e.g., Algera, 1983). Meta-analyses of these studies show clear associations between the two rating sources (Fried & Ferris, 1987; Spector, 1992).

The second set of studies have together shown that manipulations in objective job characteristics affect perceptions in the predicted manner (e.g., Griffin, Bateman, Wayne, & Head, 1987; see Spector, 1992, and Taber & Taylor, 1990, for meta-analyses). Thus, if job features are actually changed, there is a parallel change in jobholders' self-ratings.

The third stream of research stems from the social-information-processing approach to work design (Blau & Katerberg, 1982; Salancik & Pfeffer, 1978;

Thomas & Griffin, 1983) and is concerned with the effect of information from social sources on jobholders' perceptions of their work (e.g., Griffin, 1983; O'Reilly & Caldwell, 1979, 1985). Studies have been conducted that simultaneously manipulate social cues and objective job properties, with the general conclusion that social information does indeed affect employee job ratings but that these effects are weaker than those of objective job features (Taber & Taylor, 1990).

Evidence also exists to suggest that although common-method variance is clearly a valid issue, it is not the primary cause of the association between job characteristics and outcomes. Several studies have shown that observers' ratings of jobs and self-ratings explain similar amounts of variance in job satisfaction (e.g., Birnbaum, Farh, & Wong, 1986). In other words, the association between measures assessed with common methods is not necessarily greater than the association between measures assessed with different methods. The same argument against common-method variance has been made in relation to findings from laboratory and field studies. Thus, Stone (1986) reported obtaining relationships between job characteristics and job satisfaction in correlational field studies that were similar in size to those obtained within laboratory studies in which job characteristics were experimentally manipulated.

Thus, although problems can arise through the use of perceptual measures of job characteristics, evidence suggests that these are not sufficient to invalidate job design research. Indeed, a stream of research has developed in which variations in perceptions of the same objective job are considered to be a legitimate source of information. One area of inquiry, for example, concerns how people compare their jobs to others and how these comparisons affect their responses to work (e.g., Montagno, 1985; Oldham, Kulik, Ambrose, Stepina, & Brand, 1986). Oldham et al. (1982), for instance, showed that employees who carry out jobs that are seen as similar in complexity to other referent jobs have higher motivation than those who work on jobs that are seen as either more or less complex than comparative jobs.

Lack of Rigorous Longitudinal Field Studies

Perhaps the most fundamental methodological concern, and one that has not yet been adequately resolved, is the lack of well-designed longitudinal field studies that allow for causal inference (Kelly, 1992; Roberts & Glick, 1981; Wall & Martin, 1987).

Job design research has been dominated by cross-sectional studies that focus on naturally occurring variations in jobs. This is probably the weakest kind of study, and associations that are found between job characteristics and outcomes need to be interpreted with caution. One problem is that several factors might affect why people are in various jobs; thus, a link between work characteristics and outcomes could reflect these factors. For example, if different criteria have been used to select people for simplified jobs compared to the criteria used to select people for complex jobs, and if results show differences in job satisfaction as a function of job complexity, one cannot know whether the differences would have occurred anyway, irrespective of job content. Moreover, this type of study does not address whether and how job satisfaction, performance, and other such outcomes change if jobs are actually redesigned. A well-designed job is likely to be perceived differently by an employee who has experienced its upgrading through work redesign than by an employee recruited into the post (Berlinger, Glick, & Rodgers, 1988).

A somewhat improved research approach is to compare the attitudes of employees in jobs whose work has been redesigned with those of employees whose work has not been redesigned. This offers advantages over simply comparing natural variations in jobs, but it is still problematic in that the groups might differ on variables other than job characteristics (e.g., pay or attention from management).

An even better research strategy is to examine employee attitudes, performance, and other relevant factors before job redesign and then to monitor changes in these outcomes after changes to job content. Ideally, such monitoring should also be carried out for a comparison group (i.e., employees who are in similar jobs but whose jobs are not redesigned). That way, it is possible to determine whether any improvements result from the work redesign or whether they arise from other organizational changes occurring at the same time (such as increases in pay or improved communication procedures). It is also ideal to monitor the effects of job content changes over several years, not just in the immediate months after the work redesign. This is the only way to know whether effects on outcomes decline, improve, or stay the same in the long term. Useful advice about the design of applied research studies can be found in Cook, Campbell, and Peracchio (1990).

Also of concern is that many job design studies have been conducted in the laboratory using students on tasks of short duration (Kelly, 1992). Although these studies often provide advantages in terms of causal inferences because of their superior research design (e.g., the use of control groups), they lack external validity. Laboratory studies do not encompass, for example, the economic exchange aspect of working; extrinsic motivation might be a more important factor than assumed to date (Kelly, 1992). It is not surprising that comparisons between field and laboratory studies of the relationship between job content and job performance show different results (Berlinger et al., 1988; Stone, 1986).

Despite the need for rigorous research designs and the particular value of field-based studies, only a handful of studies possess both of these features (see, e.g., Cordery et al., 1991; Griffin, 1991; Mullarkey, Jackson, & Parker, 1995; Wall et al., 1986). In a review of job design research over several decades, Kelly (1992) reported finding only 31 field studies that had either a control group or a longitudinal design. The scarcity of such studies can be attributed to multiple factors, such as the difficulties of job redesign (see Chapter 7), the high demands placed on organizations of longitudinal research, and the high risk that these studies pose for the researcher (Wall & Martin, 1987).

One strategy recommended by Wall and Martin is for researchers to capitalize on "naturally occurring" developments within organizations that have clear implications for the design of work. As we shall see in the next chapter, technological developments, combined with contemporary management philosophies, mean that there is more potential than ever before for naturally occurring job redesign "experiments." We hope that researchers will take up the challenge offered by the current resurgence of interest in job design. Only by obtaining a body of evidence can the limitations of individual studies, which are bound to arise through the inherent constraints in conducting applied research, be overcome.

Broadening the Focus

Putting aside methodological issues, perhaps the biggest limitation of existing job design research and theory is its narrow focus. Traditional theory does not consider an adequate range of work characteristics, is focused on a limited number of outcome variables, does not include any aspect other than motivation as a mechanism underlying the relationship between job content and outcomes, and does not fully identify the individual or organizational circumstances under which alternative forms of work design will be effective. Here we suggest ways in which research might be constructively broadened to incorporate these elements (Table 3.1 shows a summary of our suggestions).

Increasing the Range of Work Characteristics

Most job design research has focused its attention on the five characteristics of work identified in the job characteristics model (i.e., autonomy, variety, task significance, task identity, and task feedback). However, as reviewers have repeat-

TABLE 3.1 An Expanded Framework for Work Design Research

	Focus of Traditional Job Design	*Recommended Extensions*
Work characteristics	Narrow focus on core job characteristics (task autonomy, skill variety, task identity, task significance, task feedback)	Consider a broader range of work characteristics (e.g., physical demands, physical context; social contact and support; feedback from agents; role properties; cognitive demands; interdependence; production responsibility; performance monitoring; workload and time pressure)
Outcome variables	Narrow focus, mostly on affective reactions (job satisfaction, well-being, and strain)	Consider a broader range of outcomes: Expand the range of performance and productivity indicators (e.g., include task and contextual performance); consider outcomes not suggested in the job characteristics model (e.g., accidents and safety); consider learning and development outcomes (e.g., initiative, knowledge, role orientation, efficacy); consider nonwork effects (e.g., family relationships, leisure activities)
Mechanisms		
Performance	Typically assumed that performance gains of job design derive from applying extra effort (i.e., motivational mechanism)	Consider additional mechanisms, such as the "quick response" mechanism and a learning and development mechanism (e.g., job design promotes learning, which enables operators to anticipate and prevent faults)
Well-being	Typically assumed that well-being gains are based on increased motivation and intrinsic interest	Consider a learning and development pathway (e.g., job design promotes better management of demands and a sense of mastery)
Contingency factors	Most attention to individual difference factors, especially growth-need strength	Expand the range of individual differences considered (e.g., tolerance of role ambiguity, preference for group working)

edly noted, other important features of jobs could affect employees' well-being, job satisfaction, or performance (Oldham, 1996; Roberts & Glick, 1981; Wall & Martin, 1987). Here we consider some additional work characteristics worthy of further investigation (in Chapter 5, we discuss further aspects of work that are particularly salient within modern manufacturing contexts).

Physical Demands

A feature of work that has received some attention but has not yet been systematically integrated into job design theory is that of physical demands or load (Stone & Gueutal, 1985; Taber, Beehr, & Walsh, 1985). Greater consideration of physical load would align job design research with the separate but related tradition of ergonomics (see Campion and colleagues' "biological" approach, described in Chapter 4).

Physical Context

In a similar vein, Oldham (1996) argued that physical context has been over-looked as an important job feature. One of the few studies of this kind, for example, showed that improved design of office conditions enhanced both the satisfaction and the productivity of employees (Dressel & Francis, 1987). Other studies have investigated the effect on employee reactions of spatial configuration (such as the distance between workstations and the presence of physical boundaries). Block and Stokes (1989), for instance, showed that employees working on complex tasks performed best when working in low-density conditions, perhaps because they were better able to concentrate. However, this issue clearly deserves more attention, for a later study produced a conflicting finding (see Oldham, Kulik, & Stepina, 1991).

Social Contact and Social Support

Spatial configuration is also important in that it is likely to affect the degree of social contact that employees have, possibly resulting in too much or too little contact. In a wire-drawing company, for example, social contact between team members—and hence the ability to operate as a team—was severely inhibited by the layout of machinery and the long distances between team members (Sprigg, Parker, & Jackson, 1996). Social contact and the related concept of social support have been relatively neglected work characteristics to date in work design research.

This is likely to change, however, with the recent inclusion of social support as a key job feature within the demand-control model of strain (see Chapter 4).

Role Ambiguity and Role Conflict

Role properties (notably role ambiguity and role conflict) have traditionally been examined within a stress framework but have been neglected in job design research. *Role conflict* refers to the occurrence of incompatible pressures and demands, such as requests from a supervisor that conflict with those from colleagues (Kahn, Wolfe, Quinn, Snoek, & Rosenthal, 1964). *Role ambiguity* occurs when an individual does not have sufficient role-related information to perform effectively and is unclear about what is expected (Breaugh & Colihan, 1994; Kahn et al., 1964). Both of these have been consistently identified as stressful and dissatisfying aspects of work (e.g., Jackson & Schuler, 1985), and they deserve greater attention in studies of work design. We believe that distinctions that have existed to date between job features and role properties are somewhat artificial (see Ilgen & Hollenbeck, 1991, on this topic), especially in the light of technological and other changes that are prompting a movement away from the concept of a fixed "job" to that of an emergent and flexible "role" (see Chapter 5).

Feedback From Agents

In addition to the feedback people receive from the job itself (one of the core work features in the job characteristics model), feedback from supervisors or coworkers is likely to be important (Hackman & Oldham, 1980). This type of feedback has been found to reduce role ambiguity (Sawyer, 1992).

Group-Level Perceptions

The tendency has been to focus on perceptions about individual jobs, even when work is redesigned at the group level. For example, employees are typically asked how much control they have within their job, rather than how much control the group as a whole has. These aspects, although related, are quite clearly conceptually distinct. On a day-to-day basis, employees might feel they have only limited individual control over the pace of their work, yet collectively the group might have almost total influence over pace. There is much to be gained from evaluating perceptions of individual job characteristics and group job characteristics simultaneously. One could then uncover their relative impact on job satisfaction, well-being, and performance, as well as how these aspects might interact.

Broadening the Range and Type of Outcome Variables

In line with the job characteristics model, job design research has considered job satisfaction, performance, absence, and turnover as outcomes. Most researchers using this model, however, have focused their efforts on predicting job satisfaction and other affective reaction variables, such as commitment and job strain. The effects of job design on absence, turnover, and performance have been relatively neglected. Moreover, the outcomes predicted by the job characteristics model should not be seen as exhaustive. Other salient outcomes include those relating to safety, industrial relations attitudes, and grievances; those that reflect learning and development; and outside-work effects.

Performance and Productivity

Given the resurgence of interest in work redesign as a way to facilitate competitive advantage, it is particularly important that attention be given to the issue of performance and productivity. Beyond the already-stated need for studies of this aspect that have rigorous research designs and methods (see, for guidance, Goodman et al., 1988, and Berlinger et al., 1988), we call for studies that consider a broader range of performance measures. There is a tendency to focus only on the amount produced, to the exclusion of other relevant productivity indicators, such as those relating to reduced cost, enhanced quality, greater responsiveness to customers, and flexibility. Dunphy and Bryant (1996), for example, argued that autonomous work groups "add value" in ways that are not typically evaluated (such as by making incremental improvements to work processes). There is also much to be gained by comparing the differential effects of job redesign on "task performance" (task proficiency) and "contextual performance" (helping others, etc.; Borman & Motowidlo, 1993), especially given evidence that the determinants of these types of performance differ (Motowidlo & Van Scotter, 1994). Relevant contextual indicators in relation to job redesign include, for example, task innovation (West & Anderson, 1996), "intrapreneurship" (Hisrich, 1990), organizational spontaneity (George & Brief, 1992), use of initiative (Frese, Fay, Hilburger, Leng, & Tag, 1997; Frese, Kring, Soose, & Zempel, 1996), flexibility, and adaptation to change. As yet, we know very little about how job design enhances, or indeed inhibits, these more contextual aspects of performance.

*Safety and Other Outcomes Not
in the Job Characteristics Model*

There is a need to consider additional outcomes of work redesign that are not represented in the job characteristics model, such as safety, industrial relations attitudes, and grievances. For example, with the exception of Goodman (1979), who reported that autonomous work groups led to reduced accidents, few studies have considered the impact of job redesign on safety. Yet there are several mechanisms by which work redesign and its associated changes might affect safety. Goodman et al. (1988) suggested that safe working could be enhanced because of the greater training that typically accompanies work redesign or because the removal of supervisors would mean less pressure for production. Safe working could also be enhanced because employees would have more influence over the design of work procedures and thus would be more likely to adhere to them. On the other hand, safety might be negatively affected because employees would be responsible for carrying out a wider range of tasks.

Learning and Development

Perhaps an even more fundamental and significant way to advance work design theory is to consider learning and development as outcomes of job restructuring. Thus, although we have a good understanding of how people react to job features in the short term, we know much less about how job redesign affects people in the longer term. Considering learning and development as outcomes relates to the view that human development is a continuous process extending throughout the life span (e.g., Baltes & Schaie, 1973) and to the view that personality and the environment interact to bring about change in both aspects (Cox, 1978; Endler & Magnusson, 1976). When applied to the work context, the learning and development approach has been referred to as a process of "occupational socialization" (Frese, 1982; Volpert, 1975; see also Karasek & Theorell, 1990). This is a perspective that is particularly relevant in the context of the "learning" company, which has at its heart the development of individuals and ultimately the learning of the organization itself (Senge, 1990).

Several strands of research suggest that work design does indeed affect people's learning and development (Frese, 1982). First, there is evidence to suggest that work design affects employees' *level of activity*. Studies have shown that simplified jobs can lead to a sense of resignation, apathy, and a reduced level of aspiration (Fellmann, 1980, cited in Frese, 1982; Kornhauser, 1965), and complementary research has suggested that such pacifying effects can be reversed by enhancing job autonomy and complexity (Frese et al., 1996). There is also preliminary cross-sectional evidence to suggest such effects might operate at the team level. Tesluk (1997) showed that the extent of self-management among maintenance and construction road crews was related to the extent to which the teams proactively managed their technology, such as by using preventative maintenance and by improving work processes.

Second, studies have shown that work design can affect *cognitive development*. In the best known study of this kind, Kohn and Schooler (1978), using a longitudinal data set, found that job complexity had a small but consistent effect on intellectual flexibility. (Schleicher, 1973, cited in Frese & Zapf, 1994, also reported an association between work design and intelligence.) Other studies, discussed later in this chapter, have shown that enhanced autonomy can result in machine operators developing greater knowledge about fault prevention.

A third way that work design might affect people's development concerns *role taking and the development of values* (Frese, 1982). Research has shown that people develop new role values when they enter a new job (e.g., Van Maanen, 1976) or a particular profession (e.g., medical students; Becker & Geer, 1958), and it is likely that similar changes to role values can occur when employees' jobs are redesigned. In support of this view, recent longitudinal evidence has shown that enhanced autonomy can facilitate the development of broader and more proactive role orientations (Parker, Wall, & Jackson, 1997; see Box 3.1).

The learning and development perspective on work design is informed by action theory and the demand-control model of strain, both of which we describe in Chapter 4. We will also return to this perspective shortly when we discuss how job redesign might enhance performance or improve well-being via a mechanism of learning and development.

Outside-Work Outcomes

Perhaps not surprisingly, job design research has mainly focused on outcomes within work. However, it is also important to investigate how the nature of work "spills over" and affects life outside work. Some studies suggest that employees' work experience can affect their nonwork life, such as their health (e.g., Karasek, 1990), their family relationships, (e.g., Hughes & Galinsky, 1994), and their leisure-time activities (Karasek, 1976, 1978). Nevertheless, there is too little research to provide a coherent picture as to how work affects nonwork life.

BOX 3.1. The Investigation of Role Orientation as an Outcome of Work Redesign

It has been widely argued that modern organizations require employees to adopt a new flexible and customer-focused orientation to their work (e.g., Lawler, 1992), yet there has been a dearth of research on this topic. A study by Parker, Wall, and Jackson (1997; see also Parker, Wall, & Jackson, 1994) within the context of modern manufacturing went some way toward rectifying this situation.

The researchers identified two key aspects of work orientation. First, on the basis of the literature, they suggested that employees need to develop a more appropriate *strategic orientation:* That is, employees need to accept and endorse relevant strategic objectives (such as the need for the minimization of inventory control). Second, and more important, employees need to carry these principles through to the extent that they change their view of their own work responsibilities. In other words, they need to develop a new and broader *role orientation* in which, for example, they "own" and feel responsible for work beyond their immediate operational tasks.

Following the development of measures, two field studies were conducted to examine change in role and strategic orientation. In the first study, a manufacturing initiative (just-in-time and total quality management) was introduced with efforts to inform employees through communication and training but with no attempt to enhance operator autonomy. Strategic orientation scores increased, but there was no broadening of role orientation. In the second study, a similar manufacturing practice was introduced, but this time there was a deliberate attempt to enhance autonomy by introducing autonomous work groups. In this case, employees developed not only a more strategic orientation but also a more flexible and proactive role orientation (e.g., they reported greater ownership of customer satisfaction).

Results from these two longitudinal studies therefore suggested that change in strategic and role orientation is facilitated in different ways. Whereas the former can be achieved by training and communication alone, development of a broader role orientation requires, in addition, the introduction of autonomous forms of work design.

There are many ways in which work and nonwork might interact. Oldham (1996, p. 55) suggested that if jobs are motivating, people may put more time and energy into work activities, to the detriment of outside relationships. On the other hand, if jobs are simplified, dissatisfaction may spill over and reduce satisfaction with nonwork areas. There may be particularly important relationships between work characteristics and nonwork life for women, who often report high levels of "home-work conflict"—a theme that we return to and expand on in Chapter 6 in the section "Work Design Research and Practice Implications." A further way in which work and nonwork lives might interact relates to our above discussion about the effect of work on learning and development. If long-term exposure to enriched jobs facilitates cognitive and personality development, then individuals' nonwork life may be affected in more fundamental ways. Crouter (1984), for example, showed that participation at work affected women's development more generally, increasing their desire for participation in the home. Similarly, drawing on earlier studies concerning action styles (Frese, Stewart, & Hannover, 1987), Frese and Zapf (1994) suggested that complex work environments facilitate the development of long-range goals that could then transfer to nonwork activities. Related to this perspective, some studies have shown that employees in challenging, autonomous jobs are most active in leisure and other activities outside of work (Goiten & Seashore, 1980; Karasek, 1978).

Focusing on Alternative Mechanisms

So far we have argued that there is a need to consider a broader range of work characteristics and outcomes. However, we also need to better understand how change in the former links to change in the latter. This is a question regarding the mechanisms by which work redesign has its effects. Established theory has not been very forthcoming on this issue, especially in relation to performance. It is typically assumed that performance gains are a result of increased employee motivation, but there are several other potential pathways. We believe that an especially promising area for investigation, at least in psychological terms, is the link between job design, learning and development, and performance. A similar link could also underpin the relationship between job design and well-being.

Mechanisms Underlying Job Redesign and Performance Gains

In Chapter 2, we highlighted some of the conceptual and empirical problems surrounding the link between job redesign and enhanced performance. Job satisfaction and job performance are posited to be joint outcomes of job design in the job characteristics model, yet this does not account for findings that these outcomes are typically not empirically associated (Podsakoff & Williams, 1986). Nor does it account for the well-established finding that there are stronger and more consistent relationships between job redesign and job satisfaction than there are between job redesign and productivity. We therefore need a better understanding of the latter relationship, especially the underlying mechanisms.

A Motivational Mechanism. The most common assumption is that job redesign promotes better performance via a motivational mechanism: that is, by encouraging people to "work harder" (Campion & McClelland, 1993; Locke & Henne, 1986; Wall & Martin, 1987). The motivational premise is based on need satisfaction theory (i.e., people perform better because they are doing a meaningful job that satisfies their need for growth) and expectancy theory (i.e., people expect that working hard will lead to good performance and that good performance will lead to higher-order needs being fulfilled). There are various derivations from this basic motivational mechanism. For example, one is that performance is enhanced because people in enriched jobs are more motivated and therefore less inclined to behave in dysfunctional ways, such as by avoiding boring tasks (Berlinger et al., 1988). Another is that job satisfaction (hence motivation and performance) is enhanced because employees in enriched jobs feel that they are making better use of their skills (Cordery et al., 1992).

Additional Mechanisms (Kelly's Twin-Track Model). The dominance of the assumed motivational pathway, however, was questioned by Kelly (1992), who outlined a series of associations that need to exist if the specific motivational mechanism posited by job characteristics theory is to hold. In a review of 31 field studies that met stringent methodological criteria, Kelly showed that although the relationships of job design with intrinsic motivation and job satisfaction were reasonably consistent with theoretical predictions, this was not the case for job performance. Kelly therefore suggested that determinants of job satisfaction and job performance are analytically distinct and put forward a "twin-track model" of job redesign (see Figure 3.1).

This model posits four mechanisms by which job redesign might lead to increased job performance:

1. Employees negotiate changes in job content in exchange for pay raises, leading to an agreement that fewer employees perform a similar amount of work for higher individual earnings (i.e., a "working harder" or "work intensification" explanation).
2. Job performance improves because employees perceive closer links between effort, performance, and valued rewards (i.e., an explanation based on expectancy theory).
3. Job redesign increases goal setting, and it is goal setting that motivates better performance.
4. Job redesign improves the efficiency of work methods (e.g., reducing machine downtime), and this leads to performance improvements, without any change in employee motivation (see also Berlinger et al., 1988; Hackman & Oldham, 1980).

A Quick-Response (Logistical) Mechanism. A further mechanism, not explicitly discussed by Kelly but related to Kelly's fourth point, is that performance benefits of job redesign come from enabling a quick response to problems. The

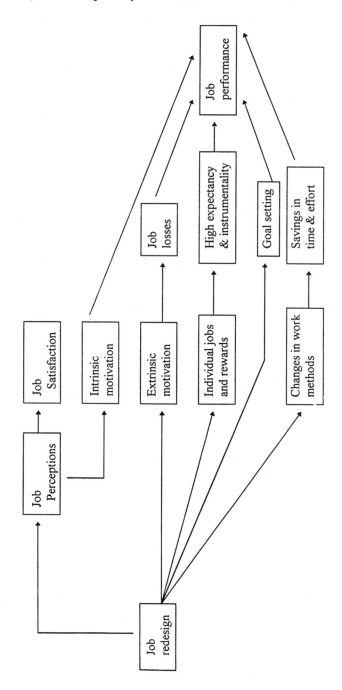

Figure 3.1. Kelly's Twin-Track Model of Job Redesign
SOURCE: Reproduced with permission from Kelly, 1992, Human Relations, Tavistock Institute of Human Relations.

premise, derived from the sociotechnical systems approach, is that controlling variances at the source (as in the case of operators fixing a machine that has broken down) will mean that problems can be solved more rapidly, with less waiting time, and more flexibly than if supervisors or specialists have to be called in (Wall & Martin, 1987). This mechanism is particularly salient within highly uncertain production contexts where there are many variances to deal with, such as those brought about by advanced manufacturing technology (Walton & Susman, 1987). As Cordery (1996) stated, "Capital cost and reliability problems associated with advanced manufacturing technology, combined with the speed with which such systems drive production, typically require frequent and rapid human intervention if the costs of deviations from ideal operating states are to be contained" (p. 234).

A Learning and Development Mechanism. Another potential pathway—one that is of particular interest to us but generally neglected in the literature—is a learning-based mechanism. We have already discussed how learning and development should be considered as an outcome of job design. However, this type of "outcome" also represents a potentially important mechanism underlying performance gain. Thus job design can promote various types of learning and development that in turn facilitate enhanced performance. Evidence for such a mechanism is most concrete in relation to the development of knowledge. Recent studies have shown that increased autonomy can promote the acquisition and use of knowledge, or "working smarter," thereby improving system performance (Jackson & Wall, 1991; Wall, Jackson, & Davids, 1992; see also Chapter 5, the section "Uncertainty, Autonomy, and Knowledge"). The same argument can be applied to the variables described earlier. Thus, employees in enriched jobs are likely to develop broader role orientations (Parker, Chmiel, & Wall, 1997), higher self-efficacy (Parker, in press), greater intellectual flexibility (Kohn & Schooler, 1982), and a greater propensity to use initiative or be proactive (Frese et al., 1996), all of which are likely to promote improved performance. Many other variables could be considered in the same vein, such as change orientation, growth-need strength, cognitive complexity, and aspiration. At the group level, relevant concepts include team-level proactivity (Tesluk, 1997) and group potency (a group's collective belief it can be effective; Guzzo, Yost, Campbell, & Shea, 1993; Shea & Guzzo, 1987).

The idea of a learning and development mechanism has been implicitly recognized for some time. For instance, Herzberg (1966) suggested that job redesign promotes psychological growth and that this involves "knowing more, seeing more relationship in what we know, being creative, and being effective in ambiguous situations" (p. 70). Similarly, in the parallel field of employee participation, Locke and Schweiger (1979) have suggested that the real potential of participation might be, not its power to motivate people, but rather its ability to facilitate cognitive growth and awareness among employees through the transfer of knowledge among people who might otherwise not share information. Recent studies lend support to this view (Latham, Winters, & Locke, 1994; Scully, Kirkpatrick, & Locke, 1995). Moreover, a learning mechanism underpins much of the contemporary management rhetoric (see Chapter 5, the section "Beyond Autonomy and Skill Use").

Mechanisms Underlying Job Design and Well-Being

It is equally important to understand how job redesign affects well-being. For example, although the relationship between autonomy and job strain is well established (see Warr, in press), there has been little investigation of the underlying mechanism. Many possibilities exist, and Frese (1989) described three broad ones. First, as assumed by motivational theory, people have a need for autonomy; thus, meeting this need will, by definition, have a positive effect on well-being. Second, autonomy can reduce strain directly by reducing the impact of stressful work aspects (e.g., having the control to shut a noisy door or to fix a faulty machine that regularly breaks down). Third, stressful aspects might remain in existence, but autonomy can decrease their negative impact (e.g., allowing someone to rest when he or she needs to might help reduce the negative effects of repetitive work). Alternatively, the negative effect of stressful work aspects can be reduced because people know they can ultimately leave the situation if it gets too bad (such as switching to another task).

A Learning and Development Mechanism. Karasek and Theorell (1990) put forward a model of work and stress that has a developmental mechanism underlying the relationship between job design and well-being (see Chapter 4, the section "Demand-Control Model of Strain," for a description of this model). The model suggests that well-designed jobs provide an opportunity for learning and, over the long term, facilitate a feeling of mastery. This sense of mastery then helps people to cope with the strain caused by the job, further freeing up their capacity to learn and develop. A similar "positive spiral" was proposed by Brousseau (1983), who argued that more autonomous jobs enhance cognitive complexity and that this "allows individuals to formulate and pursue more elaborate plans and goals, thereby enhancing feelings of personal efficacy" (p. 39). Developmental mechanisms underlying job redesign and well-being such as these, as plausible as they are, have unfortunately received little research attention to date.

A Need to Consider Contingencies

Most approaches to job design fail to specify the circumstances under which changes to work characteristics will or will not be effective. They assume general and context-free effects. It seems plausible to assume, however, that alternative forms of work design will be more or less effective under different conditions. In other words, the question is: In what way is the relationship between work design and outcomes a contingent one?

To date, the research that has taken this contingent perspective has focused on individual difference factors. There has been considerably less research effort into the question of how organizational factors affect the choice and outcomes of job redesign. As we describe next, two particularly important factors that have been identified are interdependence and uncertainty.

Individual Contingencies

It is generally agreed that job enrichment will lead to positive outcomes mainly for individuals high in growth-need strength (e.g., Berlinger et al., 1988; Loher et al., 1985; Spector, 1985). Other individual-level variables have also been considered as moderators, including work values, such as need for achievement, need for autonomy, self-esteem, and the Protestant work ethic (e.g., Ganster, 1980; Stone, Mowday, & Porter, 1977), role stress (e.g., Beehr, 1976), extrinsic satisfaction (e.g., Oldham, 1976), and job longevity (e.g., Kemp & Cook, 1983). The outcome of these studies, however, has been a rather inconsistent pattern of findings (Wall & Martin, 1987). Perhaps, as Kemp and Cook (1983) observed, rather than trying to find moderators that are replicable across situations, we should aim to "specify the conditions under which moderators are important" (p. 896).

Individual difference variables that are likely to be important moderators of work design but that have received little attention include self-efficacy, tolerance of role ambiguity, change orientation, and preference for group working. For example, because job redesign usually involves looser and more emergent job descriptions, it could be hypothesized that individuals who cannot tolerate ambiguity (i.e., who prefer more tightly prescribed jobs) will experience fewer benefits of job enrichment or autonomous work groups.

Organizational Contingencies

The area in which existing approaches to job design are least satisfactory is that concerned with organizational contingencies, especially in terms of specifying

TABLE 3.2 Work Design and Organizational Contingencies

	Contingencies					
	Technical Interdependence		Technical Uncertainty		Environmental Uncertainty	
Work design	Low	High	Low	High	Low	High
Traditional jobs	X		X		X	
Traditional work groups		X	X		X	
Enriched jobs	X			X		X
Autonomous work groups		X		X		X

SOURCE: Adapted from "Advanced Manufacturing Technology and Work Design," by T. G. Cummings & M. Blumberg, 1987, in T. D. Wall, C. W. Clegg, & N. J. Kemp (Eds.), *The Human Side of Advanced Manufacturing Technology* (p. 44), New York: John Wiley. Copyright John Wiley & Sons Limited. Reproduced with permission.

what factors affect the relationship between job redesign and performance. Cummings and Blumberg's (1987) synthesis was important in this respect. These authors identified various organizational factors that influence the choice and effects of work design over and above individual factors (see Table 3.2).

The first important factor they identified concerns *technical interdependence,* or the degree of required cooperation to make a product or deliver a service. Low technical interdependence means that there is little need for cooperation (as in the case of a personal secretary who does not depend on other secretaries to perform his or her job) and that, consequently, individual job redesign should take place. High technical interdependence means that employees need to cooperate and share information to get their job done, as in the case of one person setting up a machine and another person operating it. When interdependence is high, work should be designed at the group level so that members can coordinate interrelated tasks. The implication is that a mismatch between the form of work design and the degree of interdependence will lead to underperformance.

A second important factor identified by Cummings and Blumberg is the degree of *technical uncertainty,* or the amount of information processing and decision making required when executing the task. An operator who works on an unreliable machine that requires frequent intervention to keep it running, or that often needs to be reprogrammed because of product changeovers, would characterize a situation of high technical uncertainty. Low technical uncertainty would mean that the machine did not often need to be adjusted and that the operator rarely needed to intervene. In the latter situation, in which there are few information-processing requirements, it is argued that control can be achieved through direct supervision, tight work schedules, and the routinization of rules and procedures (Clegg, 1984; Ouchi, 1977; Van de Ven & Morgan, 1980). Simplified forms of job design are therefore suitable. In situations of high technical uncertainty, it is not possible to specify rules and procedures for all the uncertainties that arise; neither is it possible for a supervisor to make all, or the best, decisions. Decision-making rights should be devolved to operators. Control can then be achieved by evaluating outputs (e.g., by setting and monitoring goals) and by establishing norms of appropriate behavior (Ouchi, 1977).

Cummings and Blumberg (1987) made a parallel argument in relation to *environmental uncertainty.* Low environmental uncertainty is typically characterized by stable markets in which there is little change to product designs or type. In these situations, interactions with the environment can be tightly programmed, and traditional work designs are suitable. Conversely, when environments are dynamic and unpredictable, such as when the market is turbulent and product design changes are frequent, the interactions with the environment must be managed flexibly. Autonomous work designs are therefore more appropriate.

The concept of environmental uncertainty has a long history. Interest stems from Burns and Stalker's (1961) observation that the type of organizational structure that works best depends on the particular environment (see also Lawrence & Lorsch, 1969; Perrow, 1967; Thompson, 1967). Thus "mechanistic" structures, involving routinized tasks and centralized decision making, were identified as appropriate for stable and predictable conditions. However, for uncertain environments, "organic" structures that allowed flexible working and decentralized decision making were held to be necessary.

The implication from the above is that job redesign involving enhanced autonomy is most likely to lead to performance gains where technical or environmental uncertainty is high. In predictable and certain situations, although to be recommended for humanitarian reasons, the potential for enhanced autonomy to promote performance gains is likely to be more constrained. Some recent studies conducted within the context of modern manufacturing provides strong support for this proposition (see the section "The Uncertainty Principle" in Chapter 5).

In addition to interdependence and uncertainty, other organizational factors can affect whether job redesign leads to the predicted outcomes, especially those concerned with the process of introducing work redesign (e.g., adequacy of training, appropriateness of reward systems, levels of job security, management style, and method of implementation). We consider these organizational aspects in Chapters 7 and 8.

In summary, we have suggested in this chapter that although the core propositions of the job characteristics approach remain valid, the approach suffers from the problem of theoretical underspecification. This is apparent with regard to content (i.e., the restricted range of work characteristics and outcome variables), mechanisms, and contingencies. Consequently, we have put forward several suggestions to expand the theoretical base of work design. Later, in Chapters 5 and 6, we will illustrate how these ideas can be usefully applied in the context of modern organizations. In Chapters 7 and 8, we will discuss a further inadequacy of work design research that we did not deal with here: that is, a lack of attention to the process of work design and its wider organizational ramifications.

Note

1. Collectively, these can be referred to as "job characteristics theories" because they all focus on work features.

Extensions
and Complementary
Theoretical Approaches

In this chapter, we consider complementary theoretical perspectives to the dominant job characteristics approach: the demand-control model of strain, action theory, and an interdisciplinary approach to job design. We also describe models of group effectiveness that include features other than task characteristics. In many respects, these approaches serve to broaden job design research in line with our suggestions in the previous chapter.

Demand-Control Model of Strain

The demand-control model of strain (Karasek, 1979) is based on the premise that the health and behavioral consequences of work design can be predicted by

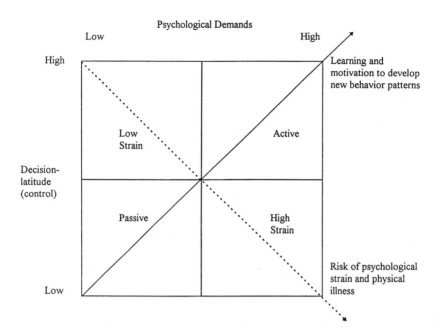

Figure 4.1. Demand-Control Model

SOURCE: Reproduced from R. A. Karasek (1979). With permission from Administrative Science Quarterly, Cornell University.

the interaction of two key work dimensions:[1] *decision latitude* (i.e., a combination of the amount of job autonomy and skill discretion) and *psychological demands* (i.e., the workload or intellectual requirements of the job). Figure 4.1 shows how various consequences are predicted by the interactions of these two dimensions.

A *high-strain job* is expected to result when there are high demands but low decision latitude, as in the case of an assembly line operator who is working under the pressure of high speed (high demands) yet has his or her behavior rigidly constrained (low decision latitude). Such jobs are considered to be the most damaging to people's health, leading in the long term to stress-related illnesses such as heart disease. In contrast, an *active job* is considered to be one in which incumbents have high demands at the same time as high levels of decision latitude. Occupations that typically fall into this quadrant include lawyers, nurses, teachers, engineers, managers, and farmers (Karasek, 1989). Karasek and colleagues predict learning and growth from active jobs, with average levels of strain. *Low-strain jobs* occur in the situation of high decision latitude and low demands, as can be the case for repair personnel. Finally, *passive jobs* occur where there are low demands and little decision latitude, as can be the case with sales clerks, janitors, and transport operatives (Karasek, 1989). It is predicted that for employees in these jobs there will be a gradual atrophying of learned skills and abilities.

There has been much research investigating the demand-control model, and both dimensions have been shown to affect strain in the predicted way. Typically, demands have stronger associations with anxiety, whereas a lack of decision latitude is more strongly correlated with depression and low job satisfaction (Spector & O'Connell, 1994; Warr, 1990). These dimensions have also been shown to be associated with negative health outcomes, such as cardiovascular disease and medical consumption (e.g., Fletcher & Jones, 1993; for a review, see Karasek & Theorell, 1990).

The most debated aspect of the model concerns the existence of the proposed interaction effect between demands and decision latitude. Although some studies have found evidence for such an effect (e.g., Fox, Dwyer, & Ganster, 1993), many others have not (e.g., Carayon, 1993; Landsbergis, 1988). Several explanations of these inconsistent results have been put forward, such as the problems of common-method variance associated with using self-report measures of demands (Kasl, 1989) and poor conceptualization of the decision latitude construct (Wall, Jackson, Mullarkey, & Parker, 1996). Although the debate is by no means resolved, it remains of interest because the practical implication of the hypothesized interaction is that as long as decision latitude is increased, one can increase demands without incurring detrimental effects to well-being.

A significant contribution of the model, which has been somewhat overshadowed by the above debate, is that its more recent versions emphasize the dynamic mechanisms by which work design has its effect (Karasek & Theorell, 1990). The expanded model (shown in Figure 4.2) depicts work design as having its effect via interactive learning and stress processes that lead to two dynamic spirals of behavior. First, regarding the idea that learning inhibits strain, the model predicts a positive spiral whereby an active job promotes learning, which reduces perceptions of events as stressful and facilitates more effective coping. Over time, these accumulated learning experiences result in a sense of mastery, or confidence. This sense of mastery then helps people to cope with the inevitable strain caused by the job and thus further frees up their capacity to accept increasingly challenging situations that promote more learning and positive personality change, ad infinitum (p. 103). Second, regarding the idea that strain inhibits learning, they posit an undesirable spiral of behavior. Jobs with high demands but low control lead to the accumulation of strain; this, in turn, means that people are less able to take on challenging situations and learn fewer coping strategies. The resulting loss of a sense mastery then further inhibits an employee's ability to cope with strain, leading to still higher residual strain levels, ad infinitum.

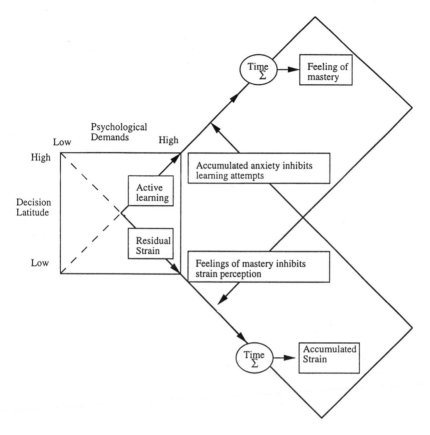

Figure 4.2. Dynamic Demand-Control Model
SOURCE: Karasek & Theorell, 1990, p. 99. Copyright © 1990 by Robert Karasek. Reprinted by permission of Basic Books, a subsidiary of Perseus Books Group, LLC.

These interesting propositions are derived from research findings, but as yet very little research has looked at the complete model and the specific hypothesized processes. Such research on underlying mechanisms will be fundamental to understanding how work design has its effects (see the section "Focusing on Alternative Mechanisms" in Chapter 3).

Action Theory and Job Design

Another approach with important implications for job design research is action theory. This theory has a long history, but one that has been largely published in German (Hacker, Skell, & Straub, 1968; Volpert, 1975). Recent articles have increased the accessibility of this theory to English-speaking countries (notably the review paper by Frese & Zapf, 1994). As will become clear, this theory has a dynamic and developmental orientation that is in keeping with that put forward by Karasek and Theorell (1990) and with that described in the section "Learning and Development" in Chapter 3.

The basic tenet of this "grand theory" is that work is goal directed, its ultimate purpose being to produce a product or service. Work is therefore action oriented: "Without action there is no change in the work object" (Frese & Zapf, 1994, p. 27). An action is defined as the smallest unit of behavior that is related to a conscious goal (Hacker, 1986, p. 73). According to the theory, there are two important features of actions. First, an action proceeds from a goal to a plan, to the execution, and to getting feedback (the "action process"). Essentially, the goal "pulls" the action and is in this sense motivational. Second, an action is regulated by cognition. This regulation of action can take place at four levels:

1. The sensorimotor level (i.e., largely unconscious processing)
2. The level of flexible action patterns (i.e., ready-made action programs, or "schemata")
3. The intellectual level (i.e., conscious problem solving)
4. The heuristic level (i.e., the metacognitive level)

With practice, consciously regulated actions can become routinized. Long-term knowledge of these processes is stored in the "operative image system" (Hacker, 1986); such systems are learned and built by acting.

The theory is substantially more complex than we have described here, although even with our brief account, it is possible to identify implications for job design research. From a practical perspective, Frese and Zapf (1994) provided a specific list of action-based suggestions for designing jobs (see Box 4.1). Many of these are similar to existing recommendations, though from a different perspective. In particular, they advocate jobs that allow "completeness of action": carrying out all steps in the action process (from goal setting to feedback) and using all levels of regulation. Actions are incomplete, for example, when there is no opportunity to define goals (e.g., because they are defined by others) or when all actions are on a low level of regulation, as on an assembly line. An action should also be allowed to "run its course," and obstacles to this (such as poor tools or a lack of information) should be reduced. Another implication is that although learning solutions to problems initially requires the highest level of skill, the situation can ultimately be

BOX 4.1. Action Theory Recommendations for Job Design

- Allow employees to choose their own work strategy (there is no "one best way").
- Ensure that work encompasses complete actions, using all the steps in the action process and all levels of regulation.
- Minimize obstacles to actions' running their course (e.g., poor tools).
- Allow people to be active in their work (as opposed to, e.g., passively monitoring highly automated machines).
- Give people control; it helps them to act more effectively, choosing adequate strategies to deal with the situation.
- Ensure that employees in well-designed jobs have good qualifications (and that the work allows them to be used).
- Qualifications can be upheld only if work has a certain complexity, so increase the intellectual complexity of the work. However, ensure that the amount of information to be kept in memory is minimized.
- Ensure that the work itself provides feedback.
- Allow job designs to continually expand.

SOURCE: Derived from Frese and Zapf (1994).

mastered and performed using standardized and automatic actions. This process means that new challenges will be needed, and job designs should evolve to provide continued learning opportunities (see Ulich, 1991, for a description of "dynamic work design").

From a theoretical perspective, an important contribution of action theory is its emphasis on cognitive processes. Thus, in contrast to the job characteristics approach, the rationale for enhanced control does not stem solely from motivational theory. Instead, Frese and Zapf argued that "people who have control can do better because they can choose adequate strategies to deal with the situation. They can plan ahead, they are more flexible in case something goes wrong" (p. 77). In other words, control facilitates a process of "intellectual penetration" (p. 43), or a deep understanding of the task and its requirements, which then differentiates "superworkers" from average workers. Volpert (1975), for instance, described how low-discretion jobs reduce people's ability to deal with problems from more than one perspective.

Most fundamentally, action theory is underpinned by the premise that "the human is seen as an active rather than a passive being who changes the world through work actions and thereby changes him- or herself" (Frese & Zapf, 1994, p. 86). Much more emphasis is placed on occupational socialization (or "personality development" in

Frese and Zapf's terminology) than is the case in traditional work design theories. A person develops his or her personality through action; thus, work has some influence on the development of personality. This perspective, that job redesign facilitates cognitive development as well as broader changes in "personality," is entirely consistent with the learning and development mechanism we proposed in the previous chapter. Parallels have also been drawn between action theory and the expanded demand-control model of strain (see Karasek & Theorell, 1990, p. 172). For example, action theory suggests that under high-stress conditions, people will favor highly automated actions over actions that require intellectual strategy formulation (Frese & Stewart, 1984). Thus, stressful situations prevent self-development and learning from occurring because they allow only a routine response. This premise is in keeping with Karasek and Theorell's hypothesized negative spiral of behavior in which it is proposed that stress inhibits learning.

An Interdisciplinary Perspective on Work Design

Reacting against the single disciplinary orientation of most job design research, Campion and colleagues developed an interdisciplinary perspective (Campion, 1988, 1989; Campion & Berger, 1990; Campion & McClelland, 1993; Campion & Thayer, 1985, 1987). These authors identified four distinct models of work design from the literature, varying in their origin, design recommendations, and expected costs and benefits (Campion & Thayer, 1985). The four approaches, including their predicted costs and benefits, are described in Box 4.2 below.

Studies by Campion and colleagues have suggested that the different approaches to job design largely give rise to the costs and benefits they propose (Campion, 1988; Campion & Thayer, 1985). However, there are methodological limitations of many of these studies, such as the overuse of cross-sectional designs, a focus on naturally occurring variations across jobs rather than on job change, and the use of self-report measures of outcomes such as efficiency. In a methodologically superior study (i.e., a longitudinal investigation of change to job content), results were shown to be more complex than expected (Campion & McClelland, 1993). Benefits were sustained in the case of "knowledge enlargement"; that is, when jobs were expanded in terms of the number of products that employees had to understand. Under situations of "task enlargement" (i.e., doing more tasks on the same product), however, there were mostly costs in the long term (such as less satisfaction, less efficiency, less customer service, and more errors). Essentially,

BOX 4.2. An Interdisciplinary Approach to Work Design

1. The *motivational approach* has its origins in job characteristics theory. It recommends job enlargement and enrichment to enhance the motivational nature of jobs. Expected benefits include enhanced job satisfaction, motivation, and job performance and reduced absence. Costs include that it may be difficult to recruit appropriate staff, that employees require more training, and that employees are more likely to experience mental overload and strain.

2. The *mechanistic approach* derives from classic industrial engineering. Recommendations stem from scientific management, time-and-motion study, and work simplification (e.g., Gilbreth, 1911; Taylor, 1911). Benefits include ease of staffing and low training requirements, but costs include less satisfied employees and greater absenteeism.

3. The *biological approach* emerged from fields such as biomechanics, work physiology, and ergonomics. The approach focuses on minimizing employee physical stress and strain (such as addressing noise limits and the ergonomic design of workstations). Expected benefits include less fatigue, better physical health, fewer aches and pains, and fewer injuries. Costs include the expenses associated with the equipment necessary to reduce physical demands and potential drowsiness from a lack of physical demands.

4. The *perceptual/motor approach* emerged from research on aspects such as human factors engineering, skilled performance, and human information processing. The focus is on ensuring that cognitive capabilities (i.e., attention and concentration requirements) are not exceeded by the demands on the job. Benefits therefore include those related to reliability outcomes (e.g., reduced error and accident likelihood) and positive user reactions (e.g., reduced mental overload, fatigue, stress, and boredom). However, a cost can be lowered job satisfaction due to a lack of stimulating mental demands.

SOURCE: From Campion and Thayer (1985).

the distinction between knowledge enlargement and task enlargement parallels that between job enrichment (see the section "Job Enrichment" in Chapter 2) and job enlargement (see the section "Horizontal Job Enlargement" in Chapter 1), a distinction that was not built into Campion and colleagues' motivational approach.

A strong point of this interdisciplinary approach, particularly from a practitioner perspective, is that it makes explicit the different underlying values about job design that are likely to be held by different professionals. It also points to the potential problems created by compartmentalizing specialists within organizations and universities, all of whom are likely to work solely within their own framework (e.g., industrial engineers in manufacturing departments, ergonomists in safety departments; Campion & Thayer, 1985). Nevertheless, perhaps as a consequence of taking a wider perspective, the motivational approach is somewhat oversimplified. It does not distinguish between types of motivational job design (such as job enlargement, job enrichment, and autonomous work groups). There is also little evidence that motivational work redesign incurs the "cost" of mental overload and stress (indeed, as described in Chapter 2, there is evidence that stress levels can be reduced). Important "benefits" of motivational job redesign have not been considered (such as faster response time to problems, employee learning, and greater flexibility), yet within modern organizations, such outcomes are likely to be more important than the traditional "efficiency gains" of the mechanistic approach. More generally, because the various approaches might suit different contexts, organizational contingencies could be built into the framework, For example, as we have argued above, the motivational approach to work design might have most benefits for performance within highly uncertain environments.

Models of Group Effectiveness

Several models of group effectiveness have been put forward that extend theoretical thinking beyond the earlier sociotechnical-systems-based conceptualization of autonomous work groups (e.g., Campion, Medsker, & Higgs, 1993; Cohen, Ledford, & Spreitzer, 1996; Gladstein, 1984; Hackman, 1987, 1989). These models differ from the more diffuse sociotechnical-systems-based approach in that they offer more specific guidance regarding how various group features link to outcomes. They also include factors not built into traditional job enrichment theory, such as consideration of the broader organizational context, the role of group processes, and the importance of leadership style.

Perhaps the most influential of these models is that suggested by Hackman (shown in Figure 4.3). This model is an example of an input-process-output model, with its core being various *process criteria* (i.e., effort, knowledge, and appropriateness of task performance strategies). Increases in these process criteria, given the presence of the necessary material resources, lead to greater *group effectiveness.* An effective group is one that meets its organizational standards, can continue working together, and meets its members' needs for satisfaction. The three levers to change the process criteria, or the *inputs* to the model, are group design, organizational context, and group synergy. *Group design* is partly about structuring tasks so that people have variety and autonomy but also involves making appropriate decisions about the composition of the group (the right number of people, a

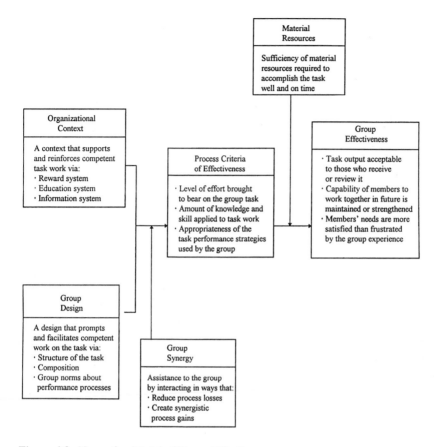

Figure 4.3. Normative Model of Group Effectiveness
SOURCE: Reproduced with permission from Hackman, 1987, Design of Work Teams, Prentice Hall, Copyright.

balance between the heterogeneity and homogeneity of group members, etc.) and ensuring that the group has appropriate norms about performance. *Organizational context* concerns having the appropriate reward, education, and information systems to support and reinforce task performance. Finally, *group synergy* is concerned with features that help the group to interact—for example, by reducing process losses.

Research regarding the predictive value of these determinants of group effectiveness generally provides support for each of the broad components. A cross-sectional study by Campion, Papper, and Medsker (1996), for example, showed that the strongest predictors of team effectiveness were various process characteristics (such as the degree of social support and communication within the team) and job design characteristics (the degree of self-management, variety, etc.). To a somewhat lesser extent, contextual characteristics, such as the degree of training and management support and the level of interdependence, were also important, whereas various composition characteristics (such as group heterogeneity) were inconsistently related to effectiveness criteria. These findings largely replicated an earlier test of the same framework (Campion et al., 1993).

Nevertheless, this study—like many others testing group models of effectiveness—suffers from some of the methodological problems that have dogged job design research for so long. In particular, there is a need for longitudinal studies that allow tests of the causality of relationships. Moreover, to stimulate more precise modeling, we advocate studies that test the specific hypothesized mediating or moderating pathways. In this latter respect, there is a need for further conceptual development (such as considering whether determinants are more appropriately assessed at the individual, group, or organizational level) to build true "models" of group effectiveness, rather than what are effectively "frameworks" that guide research.

In addition to these methodological improvements, we advocate (along with Cordery, 1996) more detailed attention to the particular ways in which groups function, such as the social processes by which decisions are made and how leadership is negotiated and exercised.

Note

1. Note that a recent expansion to the model by Karasek and Theorell (1990) includes social support as a third dimension.

5

Modern Manufacturing and the Work Design Agenda

O ur discussion regarding job design to date has been relatively devoid of the context within which it occurs. Yet the organizational environment today is radically different from that in which job design theory evolved, and this brings with it a need for a fresh perspective. In this chapter, we examine developments within modern manufacturing and highlight how job design theory needs to adapt to these changes. By doing so, we illustrate the value of the expanded research framework described in Chapter 3. From here on in, therefore, we use the term *work design* in place of *job design* to reflect the broader approach to this topic that the new context demands.

Specifically, we address two basic questions, both of which draw on our extended research agenda. First, we ask, "How do modern manufacturing technologies and practices affect work content?" This broaches the issue of whether work is simplified or enriched as a result of the modern initiatives, which has been a major point of debate, especially among those with a labor process orientation. We argue, however, that this is too simple a question and that the effects of modern manufacturing initiatives are contingent on several factors intrinsic and extrinsic to those initiatives. This leads us to the second and rather more constructive question: "What forms of work design best support the effective use of modern manufacturing initiatives?" Addressing this entails examining whether the effectiveness of work design is contingent on environmental factors (e.g., uncertainty) and exploring mechanisms other than motivational ones (e.g., knowledge-based processes). In this way, we revisit, illustrate, and add to the expanded research framework within the context of modern manufacturing.

As a necessary starting point, we describe the changes taking place within manufacturing.

Modern Manufacturing Initiatives

> There can be little doubt that contemporary manufacturing industry is
> undergoing a major paradigm shift away from the mass production regime
> that has long dominated industrial corporations world-wide. The emerging
> paradigm . . . is forcing us to completely reassess our values, our culture and
> our approaches. Kidd and Karwowski (1994, p. vii)

As the above quotation suggests, change and transformation characterize today's manufacturing organizations. Against a backdrop of global markets, political changes, and enabling technologies, companies are introducing a wide range of initiatives in an attempt to increase their competitiveness. These vary from limited one-off applications, such as the installation of stand-alone technologies, to far-reaching organizational redesign, such as business process reengineering. The scope and variety of these initiatives has led commentators to suggest the emergence of a completely new manufacturing paradigm, described variously as "new wave manufacturing" (Storey, 1994), "agile manufacturing" (Kidd, 1994), "lean production" (Womack, Jones, & Roos, 1990), "computer-integrated manufacturing" (Jones & Webb, 1987), and "mass customization" (Pine, 1993). Some commentators even go as far as to describe the new paradigm as signaling the "end of mass production" (Piore & Sabel, 1984).

Although there is much debate regarding how to characterize the transformation that is taking place within manufacturing in North America and Europe, there is less controversy about the driving force behind it. Increased competition from abroad has been a highly salient factor. At a time when manufacturing in the United States and much of Europe was in decline, Japan (and, to a lesser extent, what was previously known as West Germany) increased its export base and began to provide goods to markets once dominated by U.S. firms (Abernathy, Clark, & Kantrow, 1981). For example, the Japanese share of the world motor vehicle production increased from about 1% in 1955 to about 28% in 1988 (Womack et al., 1990).

To begin with, Japan's success was attributed to macroeconomic factors, such as favorable interest and currency rates, trading agreements, and domestic industrial policies. However, when Japanese companies began to manufacture effectively away from home, attention swung from explanations of this kind to focus on the production practices adopted by these successful companies. For example, it was observed that many difficulties experienced in U.S. companies (such as long lead times, poor quality, much work in progress, and poor use of technology), but not in Japanese companies, were problems that could clearly be attributed to different organizational practices (Hayes, Wheelwright, & Clark, 1988; Womack et al., 1990).

Two interrelated factors appeared to lead companies to success. First, with regard to strategy, the successful companies were seen as those that competed not only on the basis of low cost but also in terms of high quality and responsiveness to market demand (Lawler, 1992). The traditional beliefs in a trade-off between cost and quality, and between efficiency and flexibility, thus no longer constrain strategy. The second factor concerned the effective use of flexible production methods and technologies to support this strategy. At first, the focus was on the adoption of new programmable technology (also referred to as *advanced manufacturing technology* [AMT]), but attention has recently swung to include various other initiatives. The most well-known and widely spread practices are cellular manufacturing, just-in-time production (JIT), and total quality management.

We describe these practices and their potential to support manufacturing strategy in more detail. An understanding of these techniques and technologies is necessary before their implications for work design can be properly considered.

Advanced Manufacturing Technology (AMT)

The term *advanced manufacturing technology* (AMT) covers a wide range of computer-based technologies. Best known are those technologies used for controlling material handling and machine operation. Much AMT comprises stand-alone equipment, such as computer numerically controlled machine tools or assembly machines, and robot installations. Where pieces of equipment are integrated under shared computer control by various materials handling and transfer devices, they form flexible manufacturing systems.

AMT holds the promise of the usual benefits of automation in terms of reduced labor costs, consistent product quality, and enhanced output levels, but it has the added advantage of computer control. The latter means that work can be switched from one product to another by loading different software rather than physically resetting machines, thus enabling the efficient production of high volumes (i.e., economy of scale) as well as a wide range of products (i.e., economy of scope). In this way, a much greater diversity of products can be produced at near mass production cost, and organizations can respond more quickly to demands (Jelinek & Goldhar, 1984; Majchrzak, 1988). Two other major types of technology are important. The first is computer-aided design (CAD), which engineers use to design new products. Because it is based on a common information technology, computer-aided design also allows closer links between design and production. The second type of technology, referred to as *computer-aided production management* (CAPM), is concerned with the planning and control of production resources. For example, *manufacturing resource planning* (MRPII) is a computerized order- and material-tracking system that can improve strategic planning, allow for better monitoring and control of inventory, and provide on-line data about production schedules.

All these technologies provide potentially greater flexibility than earlier forms, especially when used in combination. The term *computer-aided manufacturing* is often used to encompass both AMT and the associated CAD and CAPM systems.

Cellular Manufacturing

In traditional manufacturing factories, the approach has typically been to organize machinery and processes in terms of the main stages of production. For example, in an engineering factory, all lathes might be in one section, milling and grinding machines in another, drilling in a third, and so on. Materials would be passed from one section to the next, routed as required to make the final product. An alternative is to group together the different types of machinery required to make a particular product or set of products into a "cell." Each cell then deals with fewer types of product, creating the advantage of a simpler work flow and scheduling, less time wasted on machine setups, and decreased work in progress or inventory.

The concept of grouping of machines in this way originally stemmed from the engineering principles of group technology (Burbidge, 1979) but has now evolved to a more widely applicable and popular method of organizing production (Littler & Salaman, 1985). Early cells tended to be single-person cells in which one operator is responsible for running several processes. Now, larger "product-based" cells involving groups of employees are increasingly common. Product-based cells involve grouping together most of the people, processes, and machinery to build a complete product or type of product. Some product-based cells even include all the necessary support functions within the cell (e.g., engineering, planning, quality inspection, purchasing), and the resulting "factory within a factory" is completely accountable for its performance. Product-based cells have the added benefit that employees can clearly identify with a given product (Oliver, 1991); thus, they are often introduced in conjunction with autonomous work groups.

Implementation of all these types of cells has been accelerating since the early 1980s, to the extent that cellular manufacturing has been described as the "quiet revolution" of British industry (Ingersoll Engineers, 1990) and elsewhere.

Just-in-Time Production

Just-in-time (JIT) became popular in the West in the 1980s and continues to be widely used (Parnaby, 1988; Schonberger, 1986; Voss & Robinson, 1987; Waterson et al., 1997; Womack et al., 1990). JIT production is essentially a system for minimizing capital tied up in raw materials, components, work in progress, and stores of finished goods to ensure that there will be minimum delay between the investment in those inputs and receipt of payment from customers (Oliver, 1991).

Traditionally, manufacturing companies have relied on high levels of inventory so as to accommodate fluctuating demand and unanticipated problems. Stocks of materials are kept "just in case" they are needed; buffer stocks exist between different stages of production so that work is always available at each stage; and finished products are stored waiting for the customer to request them. This is essentially a "push" system in which operations are triggered by the availability of materials and labor, rather than by customer demand.

The objective of JIT is to remove as much of this inventory as possible by manufacturing to order. Thus it involves a "pull" system where each stage of production is carried out "just in time" to allow the next to be completed and "just in time" to meet the customer order (Schonberger, 1986). There is a need for close coordination between the different stages of production, with minimal work in progress, because products have to pass from one stage to the next without delay. This entails the manufacture of much smaller batches, which in turn puts pressure on minimizing setup and changeover times and managing disruptions due to the supply of materials, quality problems, labor shortages, or the unreliability of technology. As such, JIT goes hand in hand with the other manufacturing initiatives, such as AMT (which reduces the setup time involved in changing over to new products) and total quality management (which helps to eliminate the need for buffer stocks to guard against quality problems), which we describe next.

Total Quality Management

The increasing importance of high quality for competitive advantage has led to a movement away from traditional quality "inspection," in which a separate group of employees inspects products after they have been made, to the design of more proactive systems of quality "management." In essence, total quality management means that quality control is no longer seen purely as a policing and rectification function but as part of a strategy in which quality is an integral part of, rather than an adjunct to, the production process (Ishikawa, 1985).

Legge (1995) summarized several essential features of total quality management theory. First, quality is not defined solely in terms of conformance to the product specification but in terms of meeting customer requirements. Second, the concept of customers is extended to include "internal customers," or the employees responsible for the next process. For example, employees are expected to develop an orientation in which they want to please or "delight" their internal customers. Third, there is an emphasis on quantitative measurement to analyze deviations from quality. Fourth, total quality management requires the involvement of all (not just quality inspectors), including senior management, employees, and external suppliers. Fifth, the concept of continuous improvement to eliminate "waste" (or "non-value-added" activities) is emphasized. The need for inspection, for example, is removed by an emphasis on making products "right the first time" (Crosby, 1979).

Many methods and techniques are deployed toward these goals, including allocating employees responsibility for quality when they are making the product, forming teams of employees who use monitoring and problem-solving tools to improve processes (e.g., "quality circles"), and changing product design to simplify manufacture (see Oakland, 1989, and Hill, 1991, for detailed accounts). There is considerable variation in the focus of total quality management initiatives, especially with regard to whether a "hard" engineering view is adopted (i.e., focused on standardization and measurement) or whether "softer" aspects (such as training and employee involvement) are emphasized (Wilkinson, Marchington, Goodman, & Ackers, 1992). What underpins the different techniques, however, is that quality structures and cultures are integrated into wider systems and "pervade all aspects of the organization" (Legge, 1995, p. 219).

An Integrated Perspective

Thus far, we have described four of the most prevalent modern initiatives within manufacturing today (Table 5.1 shows a summary of their core features).

On their own, these initiatives are not especially new or radical. What is important is the way they work in concert. Thus, AMT, JIT, cellular manufacturing, and total quality management are linked by their common potential to *integrate* traditionally separate aspects of the stages and functions of manufacturing, ultimately enabling the simultaneous pursuit of multiple strategic goals. Dean and Snell (1991) referred to this as "integrated manufacturing," a construct that is important because "it enables researchers to transcend superfluous differences among those practices and instead examine their theoretical similarities" (p. 799).

Integration can occur along several dimensions (Dean & Snell, 1991). *Stage integration* refers to the combining of the traditional stages of manufacturing (e.g., total quality management involves removing rework, testing, and inspection as separate production stages). *Functional integration* refers to the integration of manufacturing functions such as production planning, design, quality control, and accounting (product-based cells, for instance, can involve personnel from different functions working together more closely). Both of these types of integration are necessary to achieve *goal integration,* the integration or "synergy" of the three strategic goals of cost, quality, and lead time. AMT, for example, not only exploits computer control to allow responsiveness through a greater diversity of products but helps to control costs (through reduced setup times and quick changeovers) and to enhance quality (through allowing consistent production of products with tighter error tolerances).

The various initiatives also combine to allow achievement of a further strategic goal that is increasingly important in many industries: that of providing diversity and choice for the customer at reasonable prices. Many companies (e.g., IBM, Panasonic Bicycles, and Levi Strauss) are exploiting advances in technology and adopting new methods to produce and distribute tailored products on a mass basis, a strategy referred to as "mass customization" (Pine, 1993).

In summary, the new manufacturing technologies and techniques offer the promise of an integrated factory that is able to deliver the right products at the right price and at the right time.

TABLE 5.1 Core Features of Modern Manufacturing Initiatives

Initiative	Types	Underlying Principle	Benefits
Advanced manufacturing technology (AMT; i.e., a family of computer-based technologies)	Computer-aided manufacturing (ranging from stand-alone machines to flexible manufacturing systems)	Programmable technology that allows rapid changeover of products	Provides usual benefits of automation (reduced labor, consistent quality, enhanced output) Allows flexible responses to customer demands Enhances machine utilization Allows for customized goods at mass production cost
	Computer-aided design	Assists engineers with the design of products	Allows closer links with production and engineering
	Computer-aided production management	Facilitates planning and control of production resources	Improves strategic planning and control of inventory Facilitates local decision making
Cellular manufacturing (i.e., the grouping of machines and processes into cells making a product or family of products)	Can vary from a single-person cell to a "factory within a factory"	Reduces product variability	Reduces setup time Simplifies work flow Enhances operator ownership for product

Total quality management (i.e., quality as a management strategy)	Wide array of techniques, including "soft" (training, participation, etc.) and "hard" (statistical procedures, etc.)	Quality is integrated into management systems and built into the process	Promotes higher-quality products Reduces cost through decreased need for inspection and reworking Facilitates smoother work flow
Just-in-time (JIT; a system to increase the rate of throughput in the plant)	Wide range of techniques, such as setup time reduction, Kanban, and preventive maintenance	Reduces costs tied up in inventory by delivering materials "just in time" for next stage and "just in time" for customers	Lowers inventory costs Facilitates quicker responses to customers

Work Design Implications

As we have described in Chapters 1 and 2, work design theory grew from a particular context and set of work conditions (i.e., Taylorism and job simplification). However, it must now develop to reflect changes in the context and conditions. As Safizadeh (1991) stated, "Rapid technological advancements and multitudes of other changes in the environment have raised questions about the adequacy and efficacy of the existing theories of work design" (p. 63). In this section, we describe ways in which work design theory should develop in the light of modern manufacturing, drawing on the expanded framework for research presented in Chapter 3. We focus in turn on two complementary questions: How do modern manufacturing initiatives affect work content, and what types of work design best support the new initiatives?

Effect of Modern Manufacturing Initiatives on Work Content

There is much confusion surrounding the question of how modern manufacturing initiatives affect shop floor jobs. Debate on the issue has tended to become polarized around two extreme schools of thought. As with the initial studies of Taylorism and Fordism, there has been much concern that these new practices will deskill shop floor employees and reduce their discretion. The opposing view is that the initiatives will serve to enrich jobs and to enhance employee control. We describe this debate and then suggest that to advance understanding of this issue, it is necessary both to consider contingency factors that affect the relationship between the new initiatives and work content and to examine a broader range of work characteristics.

The Basic Debate: Simplification or Enrichment?

Some critical theorists have argued that the new manufacturing initiatives will deskill and intensify work (Shaiken, 1979). This school of thought stems from Braverman's (1974) original analysis of the implications of numerical control technology, the precursor to AMT. Braverman argued that such technology, by incorporating the expertise of skilled operators into the program that controlled the machinery, eliminated a key area of job control, leaving operators to simply load, unload, and monitor the machines. Braverman also assumed that management would naturally exploit this opportunity to further simplify work and enhance management control. As he vividly stated,

So far as the machine operator is concerned, it is now possible to remove from his area of competence whatever skills remain after three quarters of a century of "rationalization." He is now definitely relieved of all the decisions, judgment, and knowledge which Taylor attempted to extract from him by organizational means. (p. 202)

This concern has been generalized to AMT and computer-aided manufacturing more generally (e.g., Cooley, 1984) and, more recently, to JIT, cellular manufacturing, and total quality management (Delbridge, Turnbull, & Wilkinson, 1992; Garrahan & Stewart, 1992; Turnbull, 1988). For example, with regard to JIT, it has been argued that the standardization of processes involved leads to reduced employee discretion over work methods. Klein (1989) referred to this situation as taking away choice over "task execution," leaving discretion only over "task design." At Nissan, for instance, supervisors are expected to ensure that all operators comply with the work processes laid out in manuals. Changes to procedures can only be implemented after extensive discussion and then still need to be sanctioned by management. To illustrate the restricted discretion, Delbridge and Turnbull (1992) cited the training manual that is used at Nissan:

If the operator changes the work procedure at his discretion, he may put the process before and after that process in jeopardy, or increase the cost. . . . Therefore, *the operator should always observe the specified work procedure faithfully.* If you have any doubts, you may propose a change to the team leader and *should never change the work procedure at your discretion.* (p. 62)

A further way in which autonomy can be reduced is through the removal of buffer stocks inherent in JIT. Turnbull (1988) referred to the resulting tightly linked work flows, which mean that employees are less able to leave the workstation, as "recreating the rhythm of assembly-line pacing" (p. 13). Delbridge et al. (1992) similarly argued that with regard to total quality management, the philosophy of continuous improvement, with its constant pressure to improve processes, can take away employees' freedom to "bank" their ideas and gain idle time. More broadly, it has been suggested that the principle of satisfying the customers and their needs can be used as a way of controlling the workforce and allowing them "cosmetic" autonomy only (Delbridge & Turnbull, 1992; Klein, 1989). Initial concerns about the disempowering effects of AMT have thus continued with newer applications of JIT, total quality management, and product-based cells. These concerns are based on, and are backed up by, considerable case study evidence.

Nevertheless, in complete contrast to these views, many commentators are optimistic about the changes taking place within manufacturing with regard to their effects on work design. They believe that the new initiatives lend themselves to more complete jobs and thus "herald the end of Fordism and Taylorism" (Wood, 1990, p. 169). This school of thought is based on an "enskilling" model in which the new practices reunite conceptual and manual tasks (Abernathy et al., 1981). Some commentators believe we are at the "beginning of the end" of mass production and job simplification (Piore & Sabel, 1984; Tolliday & Zeitlin, 1986); some go as far as to predict the ultimate demise of the "job," which is seen as an "artefact of the industrial age" (Howard, 1995, p. 520) that will be replaced by flexible and emergent roles (Bridges, 1994; Howard, 1995; Lawler, 1994; Mohrman & Cohen, 1995).

The contradiction between these opposing perspectives can perhaps be understood only through consideration of the (albeit limited) research evidence. As we have described, studies exist that support both views, suggesting that neither is wholly appropriate. Moreover, some commentators are skeptical of widespread change in work design practice, in terms of either enskilling or deskilling. For example, in a study of over 100 companies, Dean and Snell (1991) found no consistent changes in the design of jobs as a result of the new initiatives. They described this as reflecting "organizational inertia," in which the tendency is not to change the design of jobs when introducing new practices. In a similar analysis of U.K. manufacturing companies, West, Lawthom, Patterson, and Staniforth (1995) reported that most companies still had simplified work designs in which employees had narrow, low-discretion jobs.

To advance understanding on the question of how modern initiatives affect work content, there is a need to move beyond rhetoric and isolated case studies to more systematic investigation. Young (1992), for example, stated that the strong views of modern manufacturing practice in the United States are "derived from anecdotes and small sample studies" (p. 678). Studies of a different type are also called for. First, there is a need for greater attention to contingency factors that might affect the relationship between new initiatives and work content. Second, there is a need to encompass a wider range of work characteristics than those focused on to date.

A Contingency Perspective

Resolution of the above debate concerning "simplification versus enrichment" is most likely to come from the recognition that both are partly right and partly wrong—that the effect of modern manufacturing on work design depends on the nature of the new systems involved, the organizational context, and the choices made in organizing work. Dean and Snell (1991) came to this conclusion: "A number of factors in an organizational context may influence the nature of factory work under the new manufacturing paradigm" (p. 795). Bratton (1993) similarly concluded that the effect of new initiatives on skill levels is not determinate because "skills have a political dimension; they are shaped and determined by social choice and a complex configuration of opportunities and constraints" (p. 397).

Research findings confirm that the effect of new practices on work content is not predetermined. For instance, although it is clear that AMT has the potential to reduce employee discretion, several studies show that autonomy can be enhanced when new technology is introduced (for a review, see Wall & Davids, 1992). The effect will depend partly on the design of the technology itself but also on the way that work is configured around the new technology. This last point is illustrated by Buchanan and Boddy's (1983) case study of the implementation of a computer-controlled system, described in Box 5.1.

Similarly, although it is clear that the potential exists for JIT to reduce autonomy, studies have shown this is not always the case (Klein, 1991). Indeed, in a recent longitudinal investigation, employees reported higher levels of group autonomy and no detriment to their individual autonomy after the implementation of JIT (Mullarkey et al., 1995). Consistent with this, Klein (1991) argued that although increasing individual autonomy might sometimes be incompatible with tight work flows and principles of standardization, the opportunity exists to enhance autonomy at the group level. Another study showed that the effects of JIT on jobs can depend, at least in part, on the extent to which operators are involved in designing and implementing the changes (Parker, Myers, & Wall, 1995). In a similar vein, Cordery (1996) summarized several studies that collectively suggest that the effect on employee well-being of quality circles is contingent on a range of factors (e.g., management commitment to the initiative).

One contextual factor that might influence the effect of new systems on work content is the degree of production or environmental uncertainty, an aspect we have discussed already (see Chapter 3). Gilbert (1996) suggested that in highly stable and certain environments, work design choices might be constrained to the design of more simplified jobs. Interestingly, some evidence supports this view. Drawing on case studies of the introduction of cellular manufacturing, Bratton (1993) concluded that work enrichment was observed only in highly uncertain environments, characterized by "one-off" or small-batch and high-value-added products. Bratton stated, "In this manufacturing environment all the managers, when faced

BOX 5.1. Effect of a Computer-Controlled System on Bakers' Autonomy

---

Buchanan and Boddy (1983) reported divergent effects of new technology on the jobs of "doughmen," who made the basic mix for biscuits, compared to "ovensmen," who baked them.

Before the implementation of the new technology, doughmen had skilled and responsible jobs. They relied on expert judgments to mix ingredients, using feedback from the sound, color, and touch of the dough to adjust the mixture. They were personally responsible for the running of their area. The new technology, however, meant that recipes were stored on programs, which activated controls to deliver the precise amount and type of ingredients to the mixing machines. The doughmen, now called "mixer operators," could no longer see, feel, or hear the mix. Nor did they need to, for their judgment was no longer required to adjust the mixture. Instead, the doughmen's job primarily involved checking the recipe program, ensuring that ingredients were available, and loading the finished mix for further processing. Thus, the new system reduced the skill, responsibility, and status of the job. "It has made it a very boring job," commented one of the managers (p. 114).

For "ovensmen," the new technology augmented feedback in a way that gave them more control over the baking process. Before the introduction of new technology, the job of ovensmen was to bake biscuits to a specific weight, moisture content, color, and so on. This was a very complex process, and the difficulty of it was heightened by the fact that ovensmen got feedback on their performance only from the later packing stage. However, the new technology involved a computer-controlled check weigh at an earlier stage in the baking process, which fed back results via a computer screen to the ovensmen. When the screen showed a problem, it remained the ovensmen's responsibility to adjust the baking process. Ovensmen felt that the technology had served to heighten their interest in the job by providing a clear goal that they could affect.

---

with a choice between skill fragmentation of skill enhancement strategy, chose the latter for operational reasons" (p. 397). In contrast, in a large-batch case, where uncertainties were fewer, there was evidence of progressive deskilling. To this end, it is interesting to note that critical theorists who have reported situations of intensification and deskilling (e.g., Delbridge et al., 1992; Turnbull, 1988) have focused their attention primarily on cases of mass production, such as the automobile industry, where the uncertainties are fewer. Uncertainty, therefore, is one factor that potentially explains the contrasting views held about the effects of modern initiatives on work that we have described. Later in the chapter, in the section "The Uncertainty Principle," we describe further evidence to support this view.

The argument that the new initiatives automatically result in job simplification or enrichment, therefore, is too simple. It is clear that both outcomes can and do arise and that the direction and extent of the change in work content depends on a number of factors, including the nature of the technology or practices, the organizational context (e.g., the level of uncertainty), the choices made in allocating responsibilities to employees, and the style of implementation (e.g., the degree of participation).

Beyond Autonomy and Skill Use

To date, we have focused on the implications of modern manufacturing for autonomy and skill use, reflecting the traditional debate. Given the established significance of these aspects of work to employee performance and well-being, they remain an important concern. Nevertheless, it is also relevant to consider whether other work characteristics are made salient by the modern manufacturing initiatives. Wall and Jackson (1995) and Parker and Wall (1996) identified the following as now deserving more attention than they have so far received.

Cognitive Demands. It has been widely recognized that modern manufacturing practices can alter the balance between the physical and cognitive demands of jobs, with greater emphasis on the latter. As Howard (1995) claimed, "In the post-industrial information age, the balance of work has tipped from hand to head, from brawn to brain" (p. 23).

More specifically, new production techniques and technologies can have two implications in this regard. One is to increase the "attentional demands," or the extent of passive monitoring, required in the job. Controlling a process via a computer screen, for example, demands a high level of vigilance (e.g., Van Cott, 1985). The other is to enhance the "problem-solving demands" in the job, such as the need for fault prevention and active diagnosis of errors (Adler & Borys, 1989; Buchanan & Bessant, 1985; Dean & Snell, 1991; Walton & Susman, 1987). In the case of AMT, for instance, it has been argued that higher-level cognitive skills are required because the new technologies absorb the routine information-processing aspects of a job while increasing the need for "employees to manage the unforeseen and non-routine variances that cannot readily be controlled by computers" (Cummings & Blumberg, 1987, p. 47). Similarly, JIT can require faster responses to problems to keep the work flowing, thus resulting in "a greater need to use initiative, solve problems and keep production going to keep subsequent processes from being starved of parts" (Tailby & Turnbull, 1987, p. 17).

It is important to monitor the effect of new initiatives of both aspects of cognitive demand. Very high attentional demands are likely to have a negative impact on employee well-being, whereas problem-solving demand adds challenge to a job. By considering the new initiatives in terms of these fundamental aspects, there is a greater chance of understanding their consequences for work design and avoiding oversimplified generalizations.

Interdependence. An additional work feature that deserves greater attention is interdependence, or the extent to which employees need to collaborate with and are dependent on each other to achieve their goals.

Having an interdependent set of tasks has long been recognized as an important prerequisite for group-based working (Cummings & Blumberg, 1987; Guzzo & Shea, 1992), and studies show that the degree of task interdependence predicts team effectiveness (e.g., Campion et al., 1996) and moderates the impact of team working on employee well-being (Sprigg, Jackson, & Parker, 1997). Nevertheless, there are still not many studies that consider the particular significance of interdependence within modern manufacturing, where new initiatives can serve to accentuate this factor. Cellular manufacturing, for example, often involves forming teams of people around a particular product who need to coordinate their efforts to meet targets. Similarly, a central feature of JIT is the removal of buffers between processes, which means that the actions of employees must be more tightly coordinated than before. The integration of strategic goals means that functional groups are required to cooperate with one another to a greater extent than is traditionally required (Buchanan & Boddy, 1982; Dean & Snell, 1991). For instance, to realize a marketing strategy of reduced lead time from order to production for a greater variety of products, cooperation is required between design, purchasing, production, and marketing (Susman & Chase, 1986).

Production Responsibility. Another work characteristic of particular relevance to modern manufacturing is that of production responsibility, or the cost of error (Wall, Corbett, Clegg, Jackson, & Martin, 1990).

It is evident that production responsibility can be greatly enhanced by some initiatives, in part because of the greater interdependence. In the case of JIT, for instance, the lack of buffer stocks between processes means that disruptions have immediate and far-reaching impact (Jackson & Martin, 1996). Similarly, AMT can enhance production responsibility because the technology itself is expensive and can suffer damage and because AMT has the capacity to produce a greater volume of output in a shorter time. Any downtime (or mistakes) that the operator causes, or could have prevented, thus carries much greater costs (Sharit, Chang, & Salvendy, 1987). This is illustrated by the experiences of a manufacturing company

BOX 5.2. A Field Study of the Relationship Between Production
Responsibility, Attentional Demand, and Strain

Martin and Wall (1989) investigated the effects of operating CNC drilling machines on
employee strain. The study involved monitoring machine operators' reactions as they
rotated through three different work conditions:

1. Single-machine operation (i.e., where one person operates one machine)
2. Double-machine operation (i.e., where one person operates two machines at the
   same time)
3. Double-machine operation with high production responsibility (this condition
   arose because the most expensive boards were always allocated to the machines
   that were operated by double-minding)

Results showed that moving from single- to double-machine operation under the
circumstance of low cost of error had no detrimental effect on employee strain. Thus,
when production responsibility was low, operators could tolerate the high levels of
attentional demand brought about by minding two machines. However, strain was
considerably higher when operators worked on two machines and experienced high
production responsibility. These findings were supported by a larger-scale cross-sectional investigation, reported in the same paper, that involved all four combinations of
high and low attentional demands and cost responsibility.

This study suggests that when an employee knows that an error is unlikely to have
important consequences, he or she can cope with the demands of monitoring more than
one machine. However, when mistakes have more significant consequences, the demands arising from double-machine minding can cause strain.

On the basis of the authors' recommendation, management in the company allowed
employees autonomy over the scheduling of their own work. This enabled operators to
plan optimally the allocation of jobs to machines, thereby minimizing their own strain
and maximizing production efficiency.

making photographic film and paper. The introduction of new technology meant
that the mixing of solutions to prepare films and paper would be controlled
remotely, via computers, rather than manually. Before the introduction of the new
technology, one operator voiced his concern: "Well, we're worried that one wrong
flick of a switch will result in thousands of pounds of wasted solutions, before
we've even had time to realize what's happening."

The importance of production responsibility was demonstrated in a field
experiment by Martin and Wall (1989), described in Box 5.2. This study showed
that a combination of high demands and high production responsibility was bad
for employees' well-being. Given the potential of some modern systems to increase

production responsibility at the same time as other demands, it is clearly important to consider such effects. An especially important question concerns whether any negative effects were alleviated by increased job control, as predicted by the demand-control model of strain (see Chapter 4).

Performance Visibility. Not only do modern manufacturing initiatives mean that employees can make more expensive errors, but they often mean that errors are more visible. Thus, modern initiatives can enhance the visibility of employees' performance, and hence the extent of performance monitoring, or surveillance, inherent in a job.

One way in which performance visibility can be enhanced derives from the philosophy of close monitoring and observation of processes inherent in modern initiatives such as total quality management. Sewell and Wilkinson (1992), for example, described a "traffic light" system of quality control in a Japanese-owned electronics company. A red card hung above the operator's workstation signaled five or more misinsertions; an amber, between five and one; and a green, none. Performance was thus available for continuous scrutiny.

Technological advances also offer the potential for increased performance monitoring. In a steel company, for instance, a device was placed in the overhead cranes to track the movement of steel throughout the factory. Employees described the cranes as "spies in the sky" and were fearful that management would use the information to isolate individuals who were not continuously working (Parker, Jackson, Sprigg, & Whybrow, 1996). Bratton (1993) described a case in which the introduction of cellular manufacturing led to "computer-controlled autonomy" (p. 395). That is, although employees were given greater authority (e.g., they had the freedom to plan work and spend money), this went hand in hand with a new control system that sent performance data directly to top management.

There can also be an increase in the degree to which employees are monitored by their peers. Delbridge and Turnbull (1992) described how production employees, in their role as "internal customers," are encouraged to identify defects and allocate responsibility to the "internal suppliers" (i.e., those employees in the previous process). Within teams, the tight interdependencies, pressure for production, and ethos of "not letting other colleagues down" can combine to give employees a sense of being monitored by their peers. Bratton (1993) referred to this as "clan control," a form of control that cannot be touched or seen but that is very powerful in its effect.

There is an emerging interest in the topic of performance visibility in the literature, especially in relation to computer-based monitoring systems (see Aeillo,

1993; Chalykoff & Kochan, 1989; Grant & Higgins, 1996). This interest, however, has not yet extended to the context of modern manufacturing. We recommend greater attention to this aspect of work, and particularly how its potentially negative effects can be mitigated (see, e.g., Bates & Holton, 1995).

Workload and Time Pressure. Several commentators have drawn attention to the increased levels of workload and time pressure that can be associated with modern manufacturing practices (Delbridge et al., 1992; McCune, Beatty, & Montagno, 1988; Parker & Slaughter, 1988). Even the sheer amount of change in an organization may lead to people feeling overloaded, as shown by this engineer's comment within a company introducing various new initiatives: "There are too many things happening at once. I feel like a juggler balancing on a high wire. I have frequent changes of priority and have to drop jobs part way through. I feel totally drained or burnt out at the end of a day."

Nevertheless, not all reports are so bleak, and some even suggest decreased time pressure and workload when new manufacturing practices are introduced (e.g., Bratton, 1993; Parker et al., 1995). We thus need to understand the circumstances under which pressure is increased or decreased. Because we know already from existing research that excessive workload and time pressure can be damaging to well-being (e.g., Karasek, 1979), it is essential to identify ways in which these aspects can be alleviated.

Generally, we need to better understand how modern manufacturing practices affect employees' jobs. The above work characteristics are among the front-runners to be considered, and there are doubtless others. The important point is that unless we approach the matter in terms of such underlying factors, we will be in danger of treating modern manufacturing initiatives as if they were all the same, when clearly they are not—with the consequence that proper understanding of their diversity, and hence their different implications for jobs, will be neglected.

Work Design to Support Modern Manufacturing

We now turn to our second question. Rather than focusing on how new practices affect the nature of jobs, which reflects a passive and noninterventionist stance, we take a more proactive orientation by asking, "How should work be designed to best support the effective use of new technology?"

The importance of this question is now widely recognized. Many studies and official reports confirm that modern manufacturing initiatives typically fail to achieve their potential and often fail outright (Hayes & Jaikumar, 1988; Lei &

Goldhar, 1993; Waterson et al., 1997). Of particular significance is the conclusion that the problems stem not so much from the initiatives themselves but more from deficiencies in the associated work design (Drucker, 1990; Hayes et al., 1988; . OASIG, 1996; Parnaby, 1988; Storey, 1994). What form of work design is indicated?

The Uncertainty Principle

There has been much consistency in the answers to the above question. Basically, following the argument developed in Chapter 3 in the section "Organizational Contingencies," theorists have reasoned as follows. Modern manufacturing initiatives, and indeed the modern environment in general, involves increased production uncertainty (such as uncertainties caused by smaller batches, more frequent changes in product design, unreliability of production machinery, and the inability to "hide" technological and organizational problems through stocks of work in progress). Because the best response to uncertainty is to decentralize decision making—that is, to allow variances to be controlled at the source—then work should be designed to increase autonomy. Thus, depending on whether it is appropriate to have individual or group designs, job enrichment or autonomous work group strategies are indicated.

This reasoning is well illustrated by Cummings and Blumberg's (1987) analysis of the work design requirements for AMT. They argued that such technology is "likely to result in higher levels of technical uncertainty and environmental dynamics" and thus that operators should be

> given the necessary skills, information and freedom to respond to unforeseen circumstances arising from the production system and its task environment, . . . the multiple skills to deploy themselves as circumstances demand, and the capacity to detect and control non-routine variances. (p. 48)

Many others have followed the same line of reasoning, generalizing it to modern manufacturing initiatives as a whole (e.g., Buchanan, 1987; Ettlie, 1988; Hayes et al., 1988; Lawler, 1992; Majchrzak, 1988; Susman & Chase, 1986; Walton & Susman, 1987). Safizadeh (1991), for example, claimed that there is a need for an autonomous work design strategy and that this is at last being recognized in practice:

> After many years of controversy and uncertainty, participative management and work design issues are becoming the focus of attention in the 1990s. Unlike in the past, however, it is not the negative consequences of extreme specialization

or the criticisms of social scientists that are spurring the movement toward abandoning rigid job design practices; rather, the movement is a concomitant to the changes in production technology and a prescription for competitiveness. (p. 62)

Certainly such a perspective is consistent with the increasing use of autonomous work groups and "empowerment" that we reported in Chapter 2.

The need to enrich work when there are high levels of production uncertainty is therefore widely supported. Indeed, rarely has there been such agreement among theorists! Certainly, we know of no one suggesting the opposite case; it is, after all, essentially Ford's argument in reverse. His alleged statement that "you can have any color of Ford as long as it is black" implies that job simplification works if one can standardize the product and thus remove uncertainty from the process. It follows that when one cannot control production uncertainty, more enskilled jobs will be more appropriate. Agreement among such diverse protagonists, however, does not necessarily mean that they are right. Moreover, there is a key assumption underlying these recommendations that ought to be challenged. This is the view that modern manufacturing initiatives necessarily entail high levels of production uncertainty.

There can be no doubt that some modern manufacturing environments are characterized by high levels of uncertainty. It is equally apparent, however, that this is not universally the case. We have already described earlier in this chapter an example of JIT applied in the automobile industry that was designed to minimize uncertainty to allow the use of standardized work methods. This is not an isolated instance. Indeed, it has been argued that the very rationale of modern manufacturing initiatives is to reduce uncertainty, such as that arising from long setup times, unreliable suppliers, and machine breakdowns (Graham, 1988). Making binding agreements with suppliers on the specification of materials along with guarantees on their delivery times, which is an element of many JIT and total quality management initiatives, is one example of how uncertainty can be reduced.

Clearly, attempts to reduce production uncertainty will be more successful in some cases than others and will depend on the environment within which the company is operating (e.g., whether the market is relatively stable or turbulent). It is also apparent that there are competing forces, some of which are likely to increase uncertainty at the point of production (e.g., changing customer requirements) and others that are designed to reduce it (e.g., continuous improvement, supply-chain partnering). In any one application, therefore, the balance between the two may be in one direction or the other, and the production uncertainty that results may be relatively high or low.

Modern manufacturing initiatives therefore differ in their degree of production uncertainty, and it follows that the work organization strategy within modern manufacturing might vary accordingly. As Wall and Jackson (1995) stated:

> One would expect the approach to shopfloor job design to vary systematically as a function of the uncertainty of a given production process, and the performance achieved to depend on the extent to which the appropriate job design approach is adopted. (p. 155)

More enriched work designs would be especially important when there is greater production uncertainty.

Two studies in contrasting settings illustrate the likely validity of this proposition. In a longitudinal study, Wall, Corbett, Martin, Clegg, and Jackson (1990) and Wall (1996) examined the impact of the increased "operator control" on the performance of computer-controlled assembly machines used to insert components into printed-circuit boards. The work redesign allowed operators greater autonomy for managing the technology, especially for dealing with any operational faults and variations in product specification. There were seven machines in use, all of which were basically the same. However, some were used for inserting larger components, whereas others were used to insert more delicate components into smaller holes. The consequence was that the machines had very different levels of production uncertainty: Those used to insert the more delicate components suffered from a much higher level of insertion problems. The change to operator control had correspondingly differential effects. For the low-production-uncertainty machines, there was little gain in performance (measured by uptime where this equated to number of boards completed), but for the high-uncertainty machines, a substantial increase in performance was achieved (see Figure 5.1).

A study reported by Cordery, Wright, and Wall (1997) showed the same effect in a different setting. Autonomous work groups were introduced in over 80 plants within the Australian water industry. There were two main performance targets: to filter the water so as to reduce the solids it contained to statutory levels (but not below, because this increased costs) and to minimize the levels of phosphates. For some plants, the nature of the technology and predictability in the levels of pollutants in the incoming water made it a relatively routine process. In others, there was much more variability to be actively managed. The results showed that over a period of 12 months before and 12 months after the introduction of group working, little or no improvement was evident in the plants with the least production uncertainty, but performance gains increased as production uncertainty increased.

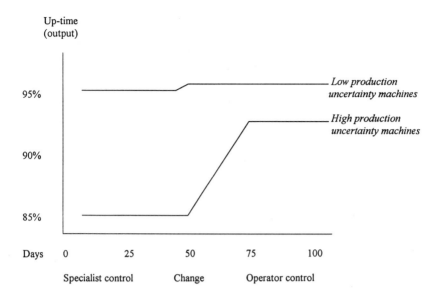

Figure 5.1. The Effect of Operator Control on the Performance of High- and Low-Production-Uncertainty Assembly Machines

SOURCE: Wall, 1996, The Psychologist. Reproduced with permission, British Psychological Society, Copyright.

In both these cases, the proposition that the performance benefit of an enriched work design strategy is contingent on the level of production uncertainty is strongly supported, whether at the level of individual or group work redesign. "Two swallows do not make a summer," nor do two studies establish the general validity of this proposition. However, there are further reasons for believing that it may be justified, which are based on understanding one mechanism through which such gains can be achieved.

Uncertainty, Autonomy, and Knowledge

In Chapter 3, we emphasized the importance of understanding the mechanisms linking work design to performance. We argued that the traditional emphasis on motivational processes was insufficient and that consideration of learning-based and developmental mechanisms was necessary. Let us consider how this might apply in the context of high-autonomy work design strategies being more effective in uncertain production contexts, specifically in relation to a knowledge-based mechanism.

It is useful to divide the argument into two parts as reflected by the following questions: (a) Why should allowing employees more autonomy promote the application and development of performance-related knowledge? and (b) Why should this have a greater impact under conditions of high rather than low production uncertainty?

Many commentators have suggested answers to the first question. Susman and Chase (1986), for example, reasoned that "aside from any motivational benefits they might derive from enriched jobs, . . . employees are in a better position to see the relationships between specific actions and their consequences" (p. 268). Operator autonomy thus maintains the "learning link" between those who detect variances and those who control them. Lawler (1992) similarly argued that enhancing autonomy promotes improvements in performance

> because employees have a broader perspective on the work process and as a result can catch errors and make corrections that might have gone undetected in more traditional work designs in which employees lacked the knowledge to recognize them. And because they have the autonomy to make on-going improvements, employees can also fine-tune and make the adjustments in the work process as they become increasingly knowledgeable about how their work can best be done. (p. 85)

In other words, the argument is that work design strategies that allow employee autonomy promote the application and development of knowledge about the work process that enables superior performance. This is a highly plausible view, for it is well established that active engagement fosters learning. Within this proposition, however, two closely related but distinguishable arguments can be discerned. One is that autonomy allows the application of existing and otherwise unused knowledge. The other is that autonomy promotes the acquisition of new knowledge.

Two field experiments provide evidence in support of these arguments Jackson and Wall (1991) further analyzed the data from the study by Wall, Corbett, Martin, et al. (1990) described earlier that showed a strong effect of operator control when using computer numerically controlled assembly machines under conditions of high uncertainty. They recognized that alternative indices of downtime could be used to test for the existence of different explanatory mechanisms. If a process of releasing knowledge was at work that related to fault rectification, then this would manifest itself as a reduction in *downtime per incident* and would be apparent immediately after the introduction of increased operator control. This would be because, given relevant knowledge, operators could respond immedi-

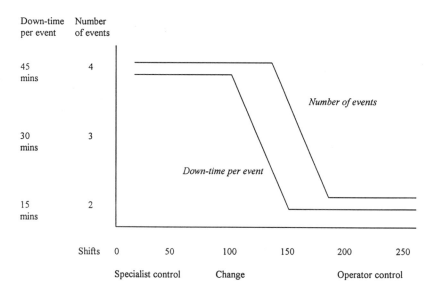

Figure 5.2. The Effect of Operator Control on the Duration and Incidence of Stoppages on a Robotics Line

SOURCE: Wall, 1996, The Psychologist. Reproduced with permission, British Psychological Society, Copyright.

ately to a problem, and faults would be remedied more rapidly than if they had to rely on remote specialists (e.g., engineers or programmers) to do the task. In contrast, a learning explanation, especially as related to the prevention of faults, would be evident from a decrease in the *number of incidents of downtime* recorded, which would become evident some time after the introduction of increased operator control. Time-series analysis favored the latter explanation. There was no statistically significant decrease in the time lost per incident following the work redesign, but there was a statistically reliable reduction in the number of faults recorded that started to emerge only some time after the increased operator control.

The problem with this study, however, is that the interpretation of the data relating to the application of existing knowledge explanation is not straightforward. Given that faults were demonstrably prevented, it is possible that those that were eliminated were typically those of shorter duration and that this masked the real effect on downtime per incident. This problem was overcome by Wall and colleagues (Wall, 1996; Wall et al., 1992) in a study of a robotics system. They tracked particular types of fault before and after an increase in operator control. As shown in Figure 5.2, the findings were clear. There was both an immediate decrease in downtime per fault and a progressive reduction in the incidence of faults.

Thus, there is empirical evidence from these two studies to support both aspects of the proposed knowledge-based mechanism for the effects of more enriched forms of work design on performance. This brings us to the second question: Why should a strategy of autonomous work design be better under conditions of higher rather than lower production uncertainty?

To answer this question, we need to consider the nature of uncertainty. Uncertainty essentially means a lack of knowledge about when problems will arise and how best to deal with them. In conditions of low production uncertainty, the course of events is predictable, and the means of dealing with task requirements are known. For this reasons, the "one best way" of carrying out the task can be determined and specified. Where there is high production uncertainty, in contrast, problems are less predictable, as are the means of solving them. This means there is more to know. Cummings and Blumberg (1987) defined technical uncertainty in terms of the amount of information processing and decision making required when executing the task. Similarly, Jackson (1989) described uncertainty as a lack of knowledge about causes and effects, or action and outcomes, within a system. This suggests that in uncertain situations, structuring work in a way that promotes learning and enables this to be applied will be both possible and important. In the words of Wall and Jackson (1995), "Production uncertainty is important as a contingency because it defines the conditions under which knowledge development and application can occur and affect performance" (p. 163).

The amount of empirical evidence available with regard to both the moderating effects of uncertainty on the effect of work design on performance within modern manufacturing and the role of knowledge and learning as an underlying mechanism is as yet insufficient to reach definite conclusions. However, the case is coherent and persuasive and is worth pursuing.

Conclusion and Additional Considerations

In this chapter, we set out to answer the question of which work design strategies best support the effective use of modern manufacturing initiatives. We sought to answer this question using general propositions that, though applied to modern manufacturing, have a wider significance. They could be used to help understand the link between work design and performance in more traditional forms of manufacturing and within other sectors and should be equally applicable to new initiatives yet to evolve. The evidence is less than complete, but on the balance of that described, we offer the following conclusions. In situations characterized by high production uncertainty, work design strategies emphasizing high autonomy for shop floor employees are likely to most benefit performance. This is so because under conditions of high production uncertainty and autonomous work designs, there is both the need and the opportunity for employees to work "smarter" so as to manage the more complex demands. Under conditions of low production uncertainty, although motivational benefits remain likely, the potential for enhanced autonomy to promote learning-related performance benefits is more restricted. Similarly, logistical benefits of work redesign (i.e., rapid responses to problems) are likely to be more modest when there are fewer uncertainties to be dealt with.

Two more general considerations, both of which were raised earlier, should be added to complete the picture. First, an additional reason, or mechanism, for the effectiveness of the autonomous work design strategy is that it also fosters the development of an appropriate role orientation, one in which people move beyond a traditional, narrow "that's not my job" perspective to a more proactive orientation in which they feel a broader sense of ownership (see Chapter 3). Second, the choice between individual and group forms of work design should depend on the degree of interdependence (Campion et al., 1993; Cummings & Blumberg, 1987). Where the effect of one person's work has direct repercussions on the work of others, a group-based strategy should be adopted, but where performance of one person has little impact on how others can do their work, individual forms of work design are most appropriate (see Sprigg et al., 1997, for a study showing how interdependence moderates employees' experience of team working within a wire-making company).

In summary, we have described how manufacturing organizations are introducing a range of new technologies and techniques to build and deliver the right products at the right time and the right cost. As researchers, we need to respond to these developments, and we need to do so using an expanded framework. First, studies are required that investigate how new initiatives affect the nature of work—an area of enquiry that will benefit from a contingent rather than deterministic perspective, as well as the consideration of a broader range of work characteristics. The second research need is to identify which forms of work design are relevant in which situations—a question that is inherently about contingencies but that also relates to the issue of mechanisms.

6

Workplace Transformations and a Workforce in Transition

In this chapter, we consider some of the wider trends in manufacturing and elsewhere that raise further challenges for work design research and practice. These changes are not clearly defined, nor do they add up to a clear overall pattern. We focus on those that we see as the most likely to draw on, and have implications for, work design. In the first two parts, therefore, we focus on changes taking place in work settings. First, we describe new forms of work that are emerging within offices as a result of information technology, such as teleworking and knowledge-intensive work teams. Second, we look at transformations that are affecting the shape of and boundaries between organizations (such as downsizing, mergers, and the development of a contingent workforce) and speculate on their implications for work design. Alongside these changes in the workplace, the demographics and expectations of the workforce itself are under transition. Thus, in the final part of the chapter, we consider some of the potential work design consequences of a workforce that is becoming "less male, less young, and less white."

Information Technology
and New Forms of Work

Recent decades have seen a second "revolution" in the world of work as a result of advances in technology. In the previous chapter, we described some of the major implications of this new technology for shop floor jobs. The implications of information technology (IT) for white-collar work, however, are just as far-reaching. Sophisticated computer systems, with ever-increasing processing power, are becoming cheaper, smaller, and more widely used. Most important, the use of computers is no longer restricted to processing and computations; computers are the new tool of information delivery (Van der Spiegel, 1995). Faxes, modems, the Internet, notebook computers, and many other systems are transforming the way people communicate with each other. Indeed, the Internet is predicted to be able to connect everyone on the planet by the year 2001 (Tetzeli, 1994).

In many respects, the debates and conclusions concerning the effect of IT on white-collar work parallel those in manufacturing. First, studies have shown mixed effects of IT on autonomy and job complexity (cf. Liff, 1990, with Huuhtanen & Leino, 1989), and there is an increasing recognition that various contingency factors can mitigate the effects of IT on work. Illustrative factors include individual difference and demographic variables, such as job grade and user experiences (e.g., Aronsson, 1989; Coovert, 1980; Huuhtanen & Leino, 1989); system characteristics, such as usability (e.g., Clegg, Carey, Dean, Hornby, & Bolden, 1997); and the management of the implementation process, such as the degree of user participation (e.g., Baroudi, Olson, & Ives, 1986).

Second, concerning the more proactive question of what form of work design will best support IT, an increasingly popular view is that work enrichment will be necessary to make the most of the new systems (e.g., Clegg, Axtell, et al., 1997; Coovert, 1995). Davis (1995), for example, claimed that "the mere possession and use of IT is not enough to ensure its success. . . . New forms of organization and new methods of managing must accompany new IT if it is to achieve its potential" (p. 112). Unfortunately, as with technological advancements in manufacturing settings, many organizations do not explicitly consider work design issues before implementing IT systems, which is a common reason that these systems do not achieve their objectives (e.g., Clegg, Axtell, et al., 1997; Majchrzak, 1988).

Although many of the research conclusions regarding office work and IT dovetail with those from production contexts, there is nevertheless a need for separate and additional inquiry. For example, although commentators recommend empowering the workforce when new IT systems are introduced, there is currently insufficient knowledge about the precise forms of work organization that will be best. It will not be enough simply to extrapolate findings from blue-collar studies; a broader approach is called for. We illustrate this need in terms of two more specific trends that arise from the increased use of IT in the office: (a) the expanded concept of "office" and teleworking, and (b) the growth of knowledge-based forms of work organization.

The Expanded Concept
of "Office" and Teleworking

A significant aspect of IT is that it enables people to share information and knowledge even though they are separated by time and space. Videoconferences and electronic mail, for example, mean that people can work together on a project around the clock and around the world (Dennis, George, Jessup, Nunamaker, & Vogel, 1988). One consequence of this is an expanded view of "office." Whereas once the "office" was a designated place in which people worked for their employers, "telecommuters" can now work from elsewhere, such as at home ("teleworking"), on the train (the "mobile office"), or even in another country (the "global office"). Indeed, people can even be physically together in a designated place (e.g., sharing desks, computers, and a secretary) but work as free agents for various organizations (Rousseau & Wade-Benzoni, 1995, p. 304). Because people are not dependent on coming into the office, they can also work a "waking week" rather than the traditional "working week" (Melvin, 1992).

The notion of an expanded "office" clearly has work design implications. Consider the particular situation of teleworking, or working from home. The core job characteristics, as well as some of the additional ones we have discussed (see Chapters 3 and 5), are likely to be relevant. For example, there is a view that, in principle, telecommuters have more autonomy over their work, especially their working hours, because there is no direct supervision and control can be achieved through monitoring outputs. However, in a recent U.K. study, many telecommuters reported that in practice their work time is tightly controlled by employer deadlines

(Huws et al., 1996). Moreover, in some cases, control is achieved through a form of electronic performance monitoring, thereby creating a potential source of strain. Reduced social contact and support from peers is a further possible outcome of working at home.

An aspect of work that has not been visible in work design research but that is likely to be especially relevant for teleworking, is home-work conflict (i.e., difficulties in juggling the demands of work and family roles), high levels of which can negatively affect well-being (Rice, Frone, & McFarlin, 1992). Although it has been claimed that working at home offers benefits such as reduced work interruptions (Venkatesh & Vitalari, 1992) and greater flexibility in balancing work and personal demands (Cauldron, 1992), there is also a potential risk of more conflict between home and work, especially for women. Huws et al. (1996), for example, reported that women teleworkers are three times as likely as male teleworkers to be interrupted by children while working. Their study also showed that high levels of job insecurity can mean that many teleworkers feel obliged to work excessive hours rather than take time out with the family.

It is clear that we need to know more about how teleworking and other forms of expanded "office" work affect the nature of jobs, including their effects on work characteristics that have hitherto been neglected, and how individual and organizational factors mediate any effects. We also need to investigate what types of work organization will best support effective teleworking. Goodman et al. (1988), for example, predicted that we will see increasing numbers of autonomous work groups whose telecommuting members are linked through computer networks. This predicted trend raises obvious questions about how such teams would operate in practice.

Knowledge-Intensive Forms of Work Organization

As we described in the previous chapter, new technology in production settings can automate routine manual tasks and increase the cognitive demands of work. The same is true of white-collar settings, such as those of research and development, sales and service, and new product development. IT often absorbs what is referred to as "routine knowledge work" (such as processing accounts) while increasing the amount of complex problem solving, or "nonroutine knowledge work" (Mohrman, Cohen, & Mohrman, 1995).

At the same time, IT has the capacity to facilitate the transfer and sharing of knowledge work, thereby breaking down traditional barriers. The notion of "boundaryless organizations" refers to groups, departments, and hierarchical levels using IT to work collaboratively (Davis, 1995). As Mohrman and Cohen (1995) stated, "Team members in different locations, on different schedules, and working in different organizations may rarely meet, but can still access the same customer data sets, use network software to do financial analyses, and share results on their electronic mail network" (p. 397). These teams are usually project based, involving temporary members who have different types of expertise. At the heart of the design of all these emerging forms of organization is the transfer of knowledge and expertise (Clegg, Waterson, & Axtell, 1996; Mohrman et al., 1995).

What are the work design implications of this trend toward knowledge-intensive forms of working? It is certainly important to continue to investigate how such forms of work organization affect job content and well-being. Mohrman and Cohen (1995), for example, suggested that because IT increases individuals' and teams' access to information (such as customer databases, markets, and financial projections), they are able to act more autonomously and make decisions at the point of action. However, the flip side is that the computer technology can be used to monitor people's performance and therefore can potentially reduce autonomy. There are thus points of continuity between this domain and that of modern manufacturing. Aspects such as cognitive demands, interdependence, cost responsibility, performance monitoring, and workload are all likely to be salient job characteristics.

Regarding the more proactive question "What forms of work design are best?" most commentators agree that some form of team working will be necessary to allow the integration of different knowledge bases and that teams should have sufficient autonomy and information to manage the uncertain and complex environment (Goodman et al., 1988; Karwowski et al., 1994; Mohrman et al., 1995). Nevertheless, commentators in the area also agree that work design theory has been derived primarily from studies of shop floor employees in manufacturing and that it will need some development and reorientation in the context of "knowledge work" (Clegg, Waterson, & Axtell, 1996; Mohrman et al., 1995).

In particular, the goal of work organization is somewhat different within these contexts. On the basis of their extensive research of teams within complex and highly interdependent knowledge settings, Mohrman et al. (1995) described how the fundamental challenge for organizations is "to design structures and processes that foster the integration of the work of people with diverse knowledge bases" (p. 66). These researchers found that the most effective teams were those that were able to use fully the knowledge of all the specialists. Achieving such integration, however, is not straightforward, for knowledge work is often carried out by people with highly specialized knowledge bases and specific "thought worlds" that derive from extensive education or training in a particular discipline. It will not be enough simply to design and install teams, these researchers argue; the work must be completely redesigned to support collective working (in other words, the aim is to create a "team-based organization"). For example, because the complexity of interdependencies within knowledge settings means that it is usually impossible to design a fully self-contained team, it is essential to design mechanisms that enable integration across the various teams.

In a similar vein, Clegg and colleagues have argued that the emphasis on knowledge gives rise to questions fundamentally different from those traditionally considered within the framework of blue-collar work. Some questions they posed were: "What forms of knowledge and expertise are designed into (and out of) work organizations? Why? How are the different forms of knowledge and expertise organized? How does knowledge and expertise get shared and developed?" (Clegg, Waterson, & Axtell, 1996, p. 247). Drawing on concepts such as distributed cognition (Hutchins, 1990), and using intensive case studies, these researchers hope to learn about the ways in which particular cognitive activities are distributed within and between people and their artifacts. In the case of software development, for example, they have argued that it is important to identify why human and social factors expertise is typically excluded, as well as to identify forms of work organization that might prevent marginalizing important knowledge. (One work design option they put forward is that of a "software development cell," based on the manufacturing concept of product-based cells, in which the team includes the full range of skills and expertise necessary to undertake a particular sociotechnical design from beginning to end.) Mohrman et al. (1995) have also called for closer links between cognitive and organizational research to identify what can be done to help people cope with greater cognitive and social complexity (e.g., they ask what groups can do to improve the collective ability of their members to process complex information, what "cognitive" tools can be developed to support collaborative decision making, and how organizations can enhance people's ability to deal with complexity).

The emphasis on collaboration and knowledge sharing also highlights the need to incorporate research from social psychology into work design theory. For example, researchers have recently begun to address questions concerning how the process of communication and decision making is affected by technology. Kiesler and Sproull (1992) found that computer-mediated communication changed decision-making processes in positive ways (e.g., there was a greater equality of participation among team members than in face-to-face mediated discussions) but also in potentially negative ways (e.g., computer-mediated discussions led to more delays and more extreme and risky decisions). Findings from studies such as this clearly have implications for the design of effective knowledge-based teams.

IT has the potential to alter fundamentally the nature of office work, not only in terms of where people work but also in terms of how they collaborate and transfer knowledge. We need to seriously address these issues, drawing on existing work design theory but also going beyond this to consider new questions that arise in the context of "knowledge work."

Organizational Transformations

As well as changes to the nature of work spurred by IT and other develop-ments, competitive pressures are prompting wider scale transformations in many companies. In particular, organizations are no longer such static and separate entities: They often change in terms of size, shape, and boundaries. This raises questions about the jobs of those employees who, for example, remain in the organization after downsizing, who are on the periphery of the core workforce, or whose companies have been "merged" or "taken over." We discuss how these various trends potentially affect, and indeed often require changes in, the design of work.

Downsizing

"Downsizing," or the purposeful reduction of labor to improve productivity (Cameron, Mishra, & Freeman, 1992), is increasingly common. One survey found that two thirds of firms employing more than 5,000 people had downsized during the 1980s (Greenberg, 1988).

Significant work design implications derive from the fact that downsizing can obviously affect the jobs of those employees who remain in the organization. However, little is known about what these effects are. Kozlowski, Chao, Smith, and Hedlund (1993) described one limitation of the downsizing literature as "the lack of research on how role changes for employees who remain in the organization affect their attitudes" (p. 282). Of the few studies that have addressed this question, the evidence is mixed. Tombaugh and White (1990) found that—consistent with views that are often portrayed in the popular press—employees reported increased role overload, role conflict, and role ambiguity. On the other hand, in an analysis of developments in mill and mine operations, Russell (1995) concluded that one of the main outcomes of downsizing has been job expansion and increased job responsibility (see also Cargille, 1995, and Bennett, 1990, for descriptions of positive effects of downsizing on jobs).

One salient distinction to make in this regard is the difference between "reactive" and "strategic" downsizing (Kozlowski et al., 1993). The former refers to reductions in the workforce undertaken mainly in response to external events and short-term need, mostly for reasons of cost-containment. Because this approach usually involves compulsory layoffs, employees who remain in the organization are likely to focus their attention more on this aspect than on the effects of any change to their work content. Reflecting the prevalence of reactive downsizing, most research has focused on how factors such as the threat to individual jobs and the degree of fairness by which the process is managed affect survivors' subsequent attitudes and behavior (e.g., Brockner, Konovsky, Cooperschneider, Folger, & Marbies, 1994). On the whole, negative effects have been recorded.

Strategic downsizing, in contrast, reflects a planned process that is in line with the long-term organizational strategy and, as such, typically involves considerable efforts to minimize negative impacts for people. In such situations, where compulsory layoffs are less common, the research questions of interest are likely to revolve around the strategic nature of change. One strategy is to develop a contingent workforce (which we discuss next). Another strategy is to become more competitive by using labor more flexibly and in more cost-effective ways. Where the latter occurs, the factors most likely to determine the effect on employees have to do with the impact of the downsizing on people's work content and with the way the change is managed.

Results from a longitudinal study have reinforced this point (Parker, Chmiel, & Wall, 1997). In a chemical processing company, a 40% downsizing was achieved over a 4-year period almost entirely through natural wastage and early retirements and was accompanied by a deliberate strategy to "empower" the workforce. As might be expected (because the same number of work tasks were distributed across fewer people), employees reported an increase in the level of work demand. However, there was no detriment to their well-being. Results suggested that the potential negative effects of high work demands were offset by improvements to work characteristics (especially enhanced autonomy, role clarity, and participation in decision making) that arose from the empowerment initiative introduced during the period. The authors concluded that, for instances of strategic downsizing, paying attention to the design of work and the wider context can enhance an organization's ability to reduce head count without incurring severe negative long-term consequences for employees who remain.

The Contingent Workforce

Within today's workforce, "employees" are no longer simply considered to be those who earn a full-time wage from the organization (Rousseau & Wade-Benzoni, 1995). There are now also "virtual" employees, such as suppliers and customers who work alongside core staff on product design and telecommuters who work from home. Perhaps most significant, however, is the growing contingent, or "flexible," workforce. Thus, as organizations try to match changing and uncertain markets, they employ more people on a part-time or temporary basis (Carey & Hazelbaker, 1986). Belous (1989) estimated that between 24% and 29% of the U.S. workforce are contingent employees.

Several descriptive models of the contingent work force have emerged (such as Atkinson's flexible firm model; Atkinson, 1985), and much research has been conducted on the meaning of these arrangements for employers, as well as on macro-level aspects (such as the supply of temporary employees). However, there has been little consideration of the impact of contingent working on individuals' jobs and well-being (Krausz, Brandwein, & Fox, 1995).

One obvious work design question relates to the quality of jobs for contingent employees. Commentators have expressed concern about the "poor periphery," not only in terms of their restricted employment rights but in terms of simplified job content (Phillimore, 1989). Recent studies support this view to some degree but show a more complex picture overall. Russell-Gardner and Jackson (1995) found that temporary employees reported less task control and lower problem-solving demands than permanent employees but reported higher extrinsic job satisfaction and better psychological health. They were also less concerned about being unemployed than permanent staff. The authors explained these results in terms of permanent and temporary staff having different psychological contracts, or expectations, about their work. In a similar study, Parker, Sprigg, and Wall (1998) found that although temporary employees had more impoverished jobs (i.e., less control and less skill variety) and greater feelings of job insecurity than their permanent equivalents, this was balanced by a lower workload and less role conflict. Overall, levels of job satisfaction and strain were similar for temporary and permanent employees.

Neither of the above studies systematically considered variations among the temporary employees. It is possible, for example, that employees in the Russell-Gardner and Jackson study chose temporary contracts (and therefore were less concerned about unemployment), whereas qualitative data in the Parker et al. study have suggested that most of these temporary employees would have preferred a permanent job (and therefore reported high levels of insecurity). Thus, a potentially important distinction is that between "voluntary" temporary employees who prefer and have chosen temporary contracts and those who are forced into temporary status because they cannot obtain a permanent position (see also Feldman, 1990). A study by Krausz et al. (1995) of female temporary employees hired through agencies supported this view. Voluntary temporary employees had high levels of job satisfaction—levels that were even higher than those of permanent employees. Involuntary temporary employees, on the other hand, reported the lowest level of job satisfaction.

A further potentially important distinction is that between temporary employees hired as individuals and those hired through agencies. These groups have a different demographic makeup and are likely to be hired for different reasons (Davis-Blake & Uzzi, 1993). Moreover, the work design implications could be different. For example, role conflict might be a particular issue for temporary employees hired through agencies, given that they effectively have two bosses, the supervisor in the client company and the supervisor in the agency. On the other hand, employees hired by an agency might feel greater job security than those hired as individuals.

Like temporary workers, part-time employees have been overlooked in research to the extent that they have been referred to as "missing workers" (Barling & Gallagher, 1996; Rotchford & Roberts, 1982). Questions concerning how to design satisfying and effective part-time jobs have yet to be seriously addressed. As with temporary employees, there are likely to be important variations among part-time workers. These include whether they are voluntary or involuntary part-time workers (Feldman, 1990; Lee & Johnson, 1991); whether they have short-term or long-standing relationships with the organization; and their degree of assimilation into the organization (Rousseau & Wade-Benzoni, 1995). For example, some employees have moved from full-time hours to part time to accommodate personal needs such as children or health and are therefore already likely to be assimilated into the organization. Others have always been, and will remain, part time and "peripheral."

The growth of the contingent workforce has not been matched by research interest. We need to know much more about the specific motivations and requirements of these employees, the effect of temporary and part-time status on work design, and how to design jobs that will promote well-being and performance for employees working under these arrangements.

Mergers, Acquisitions, and Other Boundary Changes

Like boundaries within organizations, boundaries between organizations are in many cases dissolving (Davis, 1995). Mergers and acquisitions, "spin-offs," "joint ventures," new supplier relationships, and outsourcing all involve a blurring of organizational identities.

Many of the work design implications of such transformations are likely to be similar to those for downsizing because they often involve reducing head count. Nevertheless, particular issues can arise because of the potential clash of different work design practices, systems (training, rewards, job descriptions, etc.), and cultures. By way of example, consider the case of a family-owned UK company that was taken over by their major customer, a large North American company with facilities in most countries of the world. Before the takeover, the company had made considerable moves to integrate traditionally separate aspects of manufacturing, delayer the organization, enhance employee participation, and enrich jobs. The takeover saw the transfer of several North American managers within the site who had a corporate philosophy that was more aligned to traditional mass production concepts. Moving assembly lines were installed (which meant significantly narrower assembly jobs with reduced discretion), a separate quality department was reintroduced, a special engineering department focused on process control was created, and a layer of management was added. Similar changes took place in the office. The new managers talked of the U.K.-based plant as being 4 to 5 years behind the other corporate sites in terms of "efficiency and controls." Yet the local managers and employees felt that many of the changes introduced by the new management team were "taking the company back to where it had been 10 years before." The divergent views on work design practice, which arose from the merging of two organizations, were causing considerable confusion amongst the workforce.

In the case of mergers and takeovers, therefore, it is plausible to expect that the previously separate companies will vary in work design practice, philosophy, and systems. Reactions to mergers or takeovers will therefore partly depend on how work content and the related systems are altered as a consequence.

The Changing Composition
of the Workforce

The sorts of issues we have described so far represent changes to the "demand" side of work. However, there are also changes taking place in the "supply" side.

In this final part of the chapter, we describe how demographic and social factors have led to different kinds of workers being available to assume work roles; then we consider the ways in which a changing workforce composition could affect work design practice and theory.

Less Young, Less Male, Less White

Howard (1995, p. 33) noted that the current U.S. workforce is "less young, less male, and less white" than in the past, and this applies to most Western countries. The workforce being "less young," or older, arises from various factors such as the consequences of the postwar baby boom, the general increased life expectancy of the population, a decreased birthrate, and a tendency to have smaller families. For example, whereas at the end of the baby boom in 1965, 29% of the U.S. population was over 45, by 2005 the proportion will rise to nearly 40% (Fullerton, 1993). It is thus clear that the number of older workers will increase, while the number of younger people in the labor force will decline (Warr, 1994). The description "less white" refers to the increasing cultural and ethnic diversity of the workforce, largely as a result of changing immigration patterns and higher birthrates among nonwhite racial and ethnic groups (Howard, 1995).

Arguably the most significant trend, and hence the one we give most attention to here, is that the workforce is increasingly "less male." In 1950 (around the time of the early job design studies), 33.9% of U.S. women worked outside the home (Johnston & Packer, 1987). This figure had increased to 57.8% by 1992 (U.S. Department of Labor, 1992). Similar increases have been documented in other Western countries (see Davidson & Burke, 1994). These trends reflect a multitude of developments, such as the changing role of women in society, an increase in the service industries (where women are well represented), an increase in part-time working (where women are overrepresented), an increase in divorce rates, a tendency to have fewer children, and the greater use of labor-saving devices in the home. The swing away from jobs requiring "brawn" to jobs requiring "brain," combined with an awareness of the competitive advantage of a diverse workforce, means that organizations are also recognizing that it makes good business sense to employ women (Schwartz, 1988).

Work Design Research and Practice Implications

As it stands, work design theory takes little account of age, gender, or race. Yet there are at least three important implications of the changing composition of the workforce for work design research and practice. First, we describe how there might be different relationships between work characteristics and outcomes as a function of these factors, in terms of both the strength of these relationships and the underlying mechanisms. Second, additional work characteristics or moderating variables not traditionally considered might assume greater importance. Finally, the changing composition of the workforce is likely to affect the process of work redesign.

Turning to the first of these, it is clear that work groups of different ages, gender, and ethnic status are likely to vary in terms of their underlying values and needs, which in turn will affect their responses to work design. Work characteristics could thus be more or less predictive of outcomes, and the mechanisms by which they affect the outcomes might differ as a function of age, gender, and ethnic status. Consider the effects of autonomy for older workers in physically demanding work environments. Autonomy, especially over work breaks, might be especially important in this situation—not for the usual reasons, but because it would allow older employees to rest and alleviate any physical strain. Research suggests that as employees get older, they are less willing or able to engage in heavy physical work (Davies & Sparrow, 1985). High task variety might similarly be important in reducing the strain associated with repetitive work.

In the same way, evidence suggests that men and women are motivated by different factors at work and are likely to experience different pressures—factors that should be considered in work design research. Nicholson and West (1988), for example, described evidence to suggest that women managers "have higher growth needs, and are more self-directed and intrinsically motivated in career choices" and that by comparison men are "more materialistic, status-oriented and goal-directed in their career orientations" (p. 205). Research also shows that women are also more likely to experience pressures due to sexual harassment and discrimination, being a "token" female, and being isolated (e.g., Alban-Metcalfe & Nicholson, 1984). Working women in dual-career families are also significantly more likely to experience home-work conflict (Lewis & Cooper, 1987) because they still typically have the major responsibility for domestic and child care responsibilities (e.g., Hochschild, 1989).

To date, however, from the few studies that have been done, there is not a clear picture regarding how gender affects responses to work design. For example, Mottaz (1986) found that opportunity for control had more impact on job satisfaction for men, whereas the presence of supportive supervision had more impact for women; Roxburgh (1996) reported that women were more negatively affected by high job demands and low variety than men but that there was no difference with respect to social support (see Melamed, Ben-Avi, Luz, & Green, 1995, for a similar result), and Kalimo and Vuori (1991) found no differential impact of job features as a function of gender. A study by Crouter (1994) had an even more interesting finding: Women whose jobs were enriched then expected greater participation in decision making at home, causing conflict with their spouses! Collectively, results from these and other studies suggest that the effects of gender on work characteristics and their salience are complex. It is unlikely that simple quantitative comparisons between men and women will be sufficient; research methods are needed that address the complexity of the question (including the fact that women are not a homogeneous group, for example).

The second way in which work design theory could be affected by the changing composition of the workforce is that job characteristics above and beyond those traditionally considered might assume greater importance. Returning to the case of working women with children, for example, there is some evidence to suggest that a very important feature for this group is autonomy over working hours (i.e., flexible working patterns) because it allows them to juggle more easily the demands of home and work (Thomas & Ganster, 1995). Home-work conflict, a variable that has received little attention in this respect to date, could also be an important moderator of women's responses to work redesign. For instance, one could speculate that women with substantial demands outside work might prefer more simplified jobs. On the other hand, a positive spillover could also be true. That is, women with demanding home lives might be especially keen to have, and be capable of performing, interesting and challenging jobs. The concept of "context satisfactions" (one of the moderators identified in later versions of the job characteristics model (see Figure 2.1) could be expanded to encompass "family-friendly" organizational features (such as flexible hours, child care arrangements, and parental leave for sick children), as well as the presence or absence of equal-opportunity practices.

The third set of implications of the changing workforce for work design concerns the effect of factors such as age, gender, and ethnic status on the process of work redesign. It is important to consider carefully the composition of work groups, for example. If there is a mix of ages and the work is physically demanding, a balance of younger and older employees to allow sharing of difficult duties would seem sensible. Generally, diversity within a group is considered to be good practice, although it is important to monitor the team members' functioning (e.g., ensuring that there is no harassment of or discrimination against members who are in a minority).

A further practical issue concerns the restricted opportunities for work enrichment that might arise for members of different groups as a consequence of negative stereotypes, structural barriers (e.g., home-work conflict), or other issues (e.g., language problems, learning difficulties). Women's opportunities for multiskilling, for example, might be restricted because of male perceptions about what is "suitable" women's work or because of assumptions regarding women's capabilities or aspirations. Research has shown that male managers believe that the qualities needed for management are more likely to be found in men than in women (Brenner, Tomkiewicz, & Schein, 1989; Schein, 1994), and many men still believe that women fear responsibility and leadership (despite evidence that women are just as keen for career development and advancement as men; see, e.g., Adler, 1984). Research in the United Kingdom showed that women working full time receive fewer training opportunities than full-time male workers (Martin & Roberts, 1984).

Similar issues could inhibit the full involvement of older employees or those who are members of ethnic groups. There is evidence that negative age stereotypes affect employment decisions such as training, promotions, and selection (Rosen & Jerdee, 1977) and therefore could affect the process of work design. Certainly, we often encounter managers who raise concerns about redesigning work for older employees, questioning whether these employees will be willing or able to learn new skills. In terms of willingness, older workers tend to be more involved in their job and more committed (e.g., Mathieu & Zajac, 1990), although evidence also suggests that older employees tend to lack confidence in training situations (Sterns, 1986) and, for some tasks (such as IT skills), do not learn as quickly (Sterns & Doverspike, 1989). This does not mean that older employees cannot learn (evidence clearly suggests that they can; see, e.g., Warr, 1994); rather, it means that particular attention might need to be given to training older staff when redesigning work (Belbin & Belbin, 1972; Warr, 1994).

More generally, as technological advances increase the cognitive demands of work, the relationship between age and cognitive performance becomes more salient: Will older employees be able to cope with the increasing cognitive demands in jobs? On the basis of many laboratory studies investigating this question, Warr (1994) concluded that for most tasks (such as those involving complex reasoning), there is no detriment with age; for some tasks, there is an improvement in age; and for a small number of tasks (such as those involving fast reaction time and heavy demands on working memory), there is a potential detriment with age. One implication of this research is that work designs involving more complex problem-solving skills for employees (such as continuous improvement activities) are not likely to present particular difficulties for older employees; indeed, performance of many of these tasks will benefit from their greater experience.

It is clear that systematically considering factors such as age, gender, and ethnic status will serve to make work design theory more relevant to contemporary organizations. We are not, however, suggesting that there are deterministic relationships between these demographic variables and work design. Just because employees are women, for example, does not mean that there should be an automatic focus on flexible working hours. Rather, we are suggesting that because of the changing composition of the workforce, some issues that have been historically of less importance now deserve greater attention. Work characteristics such as autonomy might be shown to affect outcomes in new and different ways, and additional work characteristics, such as flexible working hours, might become more important. The practice of work redesign, including decisions about group composition and potential barriers to equal involvement, also needs to be considered. Positive action could well be needed to ensure that equal opportunities exist for all, such as by providing computer training for older workers and designing "family-friendly" policies for employees who experience high home-work conflict.

7

Redesigning Work (Part 1): Wider Organizational Considerations

Take the following case. An electronics company was under threat from competitors due to its poor performance: Deliveries to customers were on time only about 65% of the time, costs were excessive, and quality defects were frequent. These problems were directly linked to the traditional form of work design. For example, narrow jobs meant that employees could not be moved around to deal with the bottlenecks that frequently occurred throughout the process, thereby slowing down delivery times. Similarly, because quality was officially the responsibility of inspectors, assemblers did not see it as "their problem"—a role orientation that resulted in the need for much costly rework. Management therefore decided to introduce autonomous work groups in which employees would work as a team within product-based cells (see Chapter 5, the section "Cellular Manufacturing") with a high level of discretion.

So far, so good. The company (which we shall call Electrox) has made a careful and sensible decision regarding how work roles should be reconfigured. The "team" element of the work design strategy is appropriate because it will allow coordination of the interdependent tasks that made up the process; "high autonomy" is appropriate because it will enable employees to manage the considerable uncertainty that exists within production (due to, e.g., changing customer requirements and complex technology).

Making this decision, however, is perhaps the easy part. Now begins the process of actually changing work roles and aligning wider systems, and it is here where many organizations go wrong. Work redesign initiatives that are attempted often do not succeed: They can fail to get off the ground, change can be far less radical than originally intended, change can remain limited in spread to one small section, or new work practices can eventually erode (Child, 1984). Our aim in the next two chapters is to consider the process of work redesign, particularly the implementation of autonomous work groups. Many of the examples that we give draw on the actual experiences of Electrox (a pseudonym), which we monitored as it proceeded with the redesign of its shop floor work (Parker & Jackson, 1993, 1994).

In this first chapter on redesigning work, we describe two critical aspects that need to be considered at the outset by any company planning to introduce autonomous work groups: first, how the wider organizational systems, such as training and payment, will need to be aligned to support the new work design, and second, the implications of autonomous work groups for multiple stakeholders. Later, in Chapter 8, we go on to describe in detail the mechanics, or process, of redesigning work, such as the key phases that are involved, useful tools and methods, and the critical role of a change agent.

Aligning the Wider Organizational Context

A common response to a suggested change in work roles is, "Yes, but we couldn't do that because . . ." and then a description of how the change would require a new personnel system or changes to the technology itself (Oldham & Hackman, 1980). This highlights how a change in one organizational system—the work itself—will affect or be affected by other systems. Thus, it is not possible to redesign work successfully without considering the wider context (Buchanan,

1979; Lawler, 1986; Mohrman et al., 1995; Wild, 1975). As Goodman et al. (1988) claimed, "It is unlikely that management could introduce self-managing teams into a traditional organization without corollary changes in that organization and expect them to survive" (p. 304). In this respect, being a multisystem intervention, work redesign differs from other initiatives, such as quality circles, that do not require major modifications in organizational systems (Cordery, 1996).

We discuss some of the key systems that need to be considered when autonomous work groups are introduced, including those relating to human resources, control and information, and technology (Child, 1984; Hackman, 1987; Oldham & Hackman, 1980).

Human Resource Systems

Human resource aspects, such as job descriptions, payment, training, career development, and work group selection, need to be considered hand in hand with introducing new work roles. Indeed, when autonomous work groups are implemented, evidence suggests that concerns about such aspects dominate employees' agenda. Kirkman, Shapiro, Novelli, and Brett (1996), for instance, showed about one third of people's concerns about moving to autonomous work groups were about justice, and nearly all of these concerns revolved around issues of compensation (e.g., "Why should someone else's performance affect my pay?"), performance (e.g., "Will I be appraised fairly for work performed?"), and career issues (e.g., "Will individual accomplishments be recognized?").

Job Descriptions

The basic building block of most human resource systems is the job description because it typically underpins decisions concerning selection, promotion, performance appraisal, and training. Yet elaborate and detailed job descriptions can limit flexibility and thus impede the implementation of work redesign. They directly contradict the sociotechnical principle of "minimal critical specification" (i.e., not specifying how tasks have to be done any more than is absolutely necessary). Therefore, for sustained change in work design, job descriptions typically need to be made more "fuzzy" to allow for greater flexibility (Oldham & Hackman, 1980). This process is likely to be difficult, for changing some job descriptions can require altering the whole network of interlinked job descriptions and often requires negotiations with trade unions. Even changing job titles can result in considerable resistance. In the case of Electrox, for example, specialist test engineers resisted a change in title to "product-line technicians." These support staff were expected to work as dedicated members in autonomous work groups, and they saw the new title as threatening their status and skill base (Parker & Jackson, 1994).

Payment and Rewards

One of the particularly challenging, yet critical, aspects to consider when redesigning work is the payment and reward system. An initial decision concerns whether people should be paid more when work is redesigned. One view is that people expect, and should be given, higher pay for greater responsibility, and there is some evidence that this occurs (Campion & Berger, 1990). However, in difficult economic circumstances, it is likely that any increases in pay will have to weighed against, and compensated for by, other productivity gains (such as reduced numbers of employees or staff or increased flexibility).

Perhaps even more difficult is the issue of how people are paid. Designing a payment system that promotes, for example, effective performance of a range of tasks, the acquisition of new skills, and collective effort is not easy. The relationship between payment and motivation is complex (for detailed discussions, see Beaumont, 1993; Geary, 1992; Kessler, 1995; Lawler, 1990, 1994). Three basic principles underlie most payment systems (Neumann, Holti, & Standing, 1995), all of which need to be considered when work is redesigned:

1. Payment based on the demands of a particular job or position
2. Payment based on the qualities of the person, such as his or her knowledge or skill
3. Payment for results, based on performance or outcomes (either collective or individual)

The first of these, *payment for doing a job,* is not likely to be sensible when work is enriched. Lawler (1990) described how a system focusing on people rather than jobs is more appropriate: "In today's rapidly changing and highly competitive environment, a message that says grow, develop and perform well seems to be more on target than one that says you will be rewarded for outgrowing your job and getting promoted" (p. 142).

Nevertheless, despite the "good sense" of Lawler's statement, most companies have not abandoned job evaluation schemes, although they are modifying them in important ways (Kessler, 1995). To promote flexibility, many companies have simplified the grading structures by reducing the number of grades and creating broader bands (integrating manual and white-collar work into the same bands in some cases). Other ways that job evaluation schemes have been adapted include basing movement between levels on professional qualifications or the acquisition of skills or competencies (rather than solely on seniority or promotion), developing group-based evaluation systems in which team members are equally paid for undertaking a set of tasks (Neumann et al., 1995), and developing grades that have a minimum and maximum, allowing scope for payment on the basis of skills or performance.

Payment on the basis of people's skills or knowledge is an increasingly popular method when there have been work design changes (Beaumont, 1993; Kessler, 1995). The idea is that paying people on the basis of skills they acquire (or that the team acquires, in some cases) will promote flexibility and skill development (Lawler, 1990, 1994; Mohrman et al., 1995). Although fine in theory, there are some problems with a skill-based approach, including that the system can promote too much generalization within teams; people can get frustrated when they reach the top of the skill ladder; the wage bill can become unsustainable if everyone attains skill targets; payment for skills that are not wanted or unused is costly; and supervisors can be reluctant to release people for training (Beaumont, 1993; Neumann et al., 1995). Proactive steps need to be taken to address these issues if such a scheme is to be successful, such as ensuring that employees have realistic expectations about the pace and extent of skill acquisition.

Another popular alternative is *payment on the basis of people's performance* (Kanter, 1989). Examples include individual piecework, payment by results, merit pay, group bonuses, and payment linked to organizational performance. In theory, such schemes will promote achievement on the relevant outcomes. In practice, performance-related payment schemes are often controversial and receive only minimal acceptance from employees (Lawler, 1990). A minimum requirement is to ensure that outcomes can be influenced by the group or individual. It should also be possible to measure performance clearly and fairly (this might require training of supervisors in the appraisal process), and employees need to trust management and the figures that they present (Beaumont, 1993; Oldham & Hackman, 1980). Neumann et al. (1995) suggested that the performance-related pay component should be at least 3% of an overall package to act as an incentive.

Certainly, *individual bonus schemes* (such as piecework) will be inappropriate when work is redesigned, for they inhibit flexibility and promote a narrow, extrinsic work orientation. Even if the assessment of performance is based on broader criteria, individual performance-related schemes do not coexist that well with team working and can encourage competitive relationships between employees (Lawler,

1990). At the very least, if individual appraisal systems are used, one should ensure that the criteria include a collective component. Electrox, for instance, modified their existing appraisal system to include criteria such as breadth and depth of skills, product ownership, and team-working behavior (see Parker, Mullarkey, & Jackson, 1994, on this topic). An extension of this principle would be to have peers (or even customers) assess the team-oriented components of appraisals, rather than to rely solely on the assessments of the group leader or manager.

Team-based bonuses (i.e., such that the group is rewarded on the basis of its performance) are an alternative (Grey & Corlett, 1989; Lawler, 1981), and there is some evidence to suggest such systems promote better team and business unit performance than individual reward systems (Mohrman et al., 1995). Nevertheless, team-based rewards systems can be difficult to set up (teams should have equal opportunities to achieve bonuses), and they can promote unproductive competition. Moreover, if employees perceive that they work harder than their peers but are paid the same, they are likely to perceive pay inequity or distributive injustice (Adams, 1965). Even with a group-based payment system, there is value in having a mechanism to reward individuals according to their skill levels, responsibility, or performance (e.g., Grey & Corlett, 1989). Mohrman et al. (1995) argued that although team-based performance schemes are often seen as unfair to begin with, a logic shift occurs with experience of team working, and people come to accept them.

Organizationwide performance-related pay systems (such as a companywide bonus or profit-related pay) are likely to be most effective when cooperation is necessary among all employees or when the contributions of individuals or groups to organizational performance cannot be separated (Oldham & Hackman, 1980). Hatcher and Ross (1991) described a case study in which the introduction of plantwide bonuses (i.e., gainsharing plans) resulted in improved team working and enhanced performance. Other options are to combine an organizationwide scheme with other payment schemes and to allow employees to buy shares in the company.

At the end of the day, because there is no universal "best practice" payment system (Beaumont, 1993; Lawler, 1994), organizations will need to combine a mixture of elements to achieve a system appropriate for their situation. One company's payment scheme to support autonomous work groups had four segments: one based on achieving basic job proficiency, one based on the degree of flexibility and self-regulation of the team (i.e., a team-based pay-for-skills system), one based on individual skills over and above what was required in the team, and one based on company-level performance (Neumann et al., 1995, p. 216). Redesign of payment systems will also need to take account of existing custom and practice, such as inequities in wages that might be a residue from previous payment systems, and expectations regarding overtime. In a chemical company that redesigned work into teams, for instance, the offer of staff status and its accompanying benefits was used as part of a complex trade-off between gains and losses, including overtime (Neumann et al., 1995). Finally, the reward system may well need to be recalibrated as expectations and requirements change (Goodman & Dean, 1982; Mohrman et al., 1995).

Training Practice and Systems

Training is highlighted with work redesign because a wider skill base is required (especially if there is a skill-based payment system). As well as training employees in technical aspects, however, they will also benefit from training in team-working and decision-making skills (Grey & Corlett, 1989; Liebowitz & DeMeuse, 1982), business understanding (Lawler, 1992), and performance management and goal-setting skills (Stevens & Campion, 1994). For many employees, activities such as attending meetings, solving long-term problems, and working collaboratively will be new work experiences, and training can enhance employee confidence and skills in these competencies. Training will also be necessary for supervisors of support staff if they are expected to take on new roles.

Although the need for training is clear, many organizations (such as Electrox) significantly underestimate the training requirements of work redesign and fail to put in place appropriate systems and practices to support the higher training demands (such as skill matrices, skill certification processes, and training needs analyses). Companies also need to be aware that training needs extend beyond the start-up phase and that people will need to be taught skills that help the group develop over time (Goodman & Dean, 1982). In this respect, many companies engage in "team-building" training to enhance team cohesiveness and functioning. Typically, this involves team members' engaging in off-site activities that explicitly require cooperation and knowledge sharing (such as orienteering). Ultimately, however, such team-building training is valuable only if mechanisms are put in place to ensure that new knowledge, skills, or attitudes are transferred back to the workplace.

Career Development

There are at least two broad implications of work redesign for career development (Oldham & Hackman, 1980). The first is that some employees might be overstretched by their new jobs, resulting in raised anxiety, absence, or other negative outcomes (Turner & Lawrence, 1965). Such reactions can be temporary, arising because years of simplified jobs can engender among employees a sense of "learned helplessness" and passivity (Argyris, 1964; Parker, 1996). Nevertheless, some allowance also needs to be made for those employees who, even in the long term, prefer, or are only capable of, less challenging work (e.g., allowing them to choose the easier tasks within a group or moving them to specially created positions). Consideration also needs to be given to employees who are unable to adapt to group forms of working, and the provision of counseling has been suggested as a minimum requirement (Neumann et al., 1995).

A second career implication concerns the design of systems for personal advancement. Employees in redesigned work can "top out," or become so stimulated by the work that they seek additional responsibilities that are no longer readily available. With greater responsibility devolved to shop floor employees, there is often the need for fewer supervisors and managers, and thus the traditional promotional ladder is more limited. This issue highlights the importance of allowing job designs to continue to expand (see Chapter 3) but also signals the need to devise other career development options, such as encouraging "sideways" development (e.g., learning different technical skills) or offering special assignments (e.g., short-term challenging projects). People need to reconceptualize their view of careers away from "hierarchical progression"—a change in mentality that is difficult to achieve and that will certainly require reward systems that encourage sideways development (Lawler, 1990; Mohrman et al., 1995).

Selection and Recruitment

Neuman (1991) argued that the requirements for working in autonomous groups are so different from those traditionally required that it is necessary to specially select employees for this type of work organization. Certainly, we would advocate such selection if it is feasible, but we recognize that it is often not appropriate—at least in the short term—within brownfield sites. Over the longer term, however, changes to selection and recruitment systems will be necessary if the work redesign program is to develop. Alternative selection criteria will need to complement, or replace, the use of traditional technically based criteria. Lawler (1994) argued that people should be selected for organizational membership (particularly for their ability to learn) rather than for a specific job. Methods appropriate to selecting the right people (such as cognitive tests, assessment centers, or work samples) will need to be put in place, and it is important to design mechanisms to allow existing employees input into decisions regarding who is selected for their team.

Control and Information Systems

In the same way that human resource systems need to be aligned with the work redesign, so too do control and information systems. Control systems include any mechanical systems that are designed to control employee behavior in an automatic fashion (Oldham & Hackman, 1980, p. 255). Examples include budget and cost accounting methods; production reports; purchasing, sales, and marketing practices; attendance measuring devices; and electronic monitoring systems. Such control systems can constrain the redesign of jobs, as illustrated by the situation in a chemical processing plant in which employees in autonomous work groups were not able to obtain their own basic protective equipment because a manager's signature was required on all order requests. Another example was shown in an engineering company in which, because key measures of performance were based on machine use, supervisors did not allow operators to train on other machines so as not to incur the short-term costs of reduced running time.

Information systems can similarly serve to constrain the opportunity for enhanced autonomy, especially because they are often designed with simplified jobs in mind (Clegg & Fitter, 1978; Emery, 1980; Grey & Corlett, 1989). Scherer and Weik (1996) described a case in which the centralized production information system conflicted with the need for empowered shop floor teams to make local decisions. The system was then restructured so that instead of being told what to do, operators received information that allowed them to make their own planning decisions. Generally, systems need to be designed so that employees have the necessary information to act on problems that arise, make decisions, interact effectively with other groups, and continuously learn from their mistakes. As Cherns (1987) stated,

> It is no use holding an individual or team responsible for any function and doling out information about its performance in arrears and through a higher authority. Under those conditions, the individual or team cannot have ownership of its performance. (p. 157)

Technological advances in data processing, such as MRP and MRP II, if used correctly, can facilitate the extent to which employees receive timely information about their performance. Employees will also need access to strategic information (such as company goals, customer requirements, and who competitors are); otherwise, they cannot be expected to carry out the broader activities required with autonomous working, such as liaison with customers, setting targets, and deciding priorities.

No matter how necessary, changing control and information systems can be tough. Some of the problems are that these systems often involve substantial investment in sophisticated technology; people involved in maintaining the systems can feel threatened by attempts to redesign them; and changes can sometimes be illegal or can affect companies' contracts with their customers, as in the case of changing quality control systems. Regarding the latter, for example, operators in one company could not inspect steel bars because the customer award of quality control was dependent on using "examiners" who had to attend a lengthy and costly external training course.

Technology

To date, we have taken for granted that work redesign is feasible. However, with some types of technology, it is difficult (and some argue, impossible) to build in a meaningful amount of autonomy, variety, or feedback. With a moving assembly line, for example, the work pace is controlled by the line itself, and the breadth of tasks is severely restricted by its very design (Blauner, 1964; Walker & Guest, 1952). Indeed, that is its *raison d'être*. With such technologies, it has been suggested that efforts to enrich work are "doomed to failure from the outset because of the mechanics of the system itself" (Oldham & Hackman, 1980, p. 253). Work design can also be constrained in less extreme ways—for example, when plant and equipment layout is arranged in formats, such as the functional organization of processes, that are incompatible with natural work groups (see Chapter 5, the section "Cellular Manufacturing").

If work is to be meaningfully reorganized, therefore, either the technology must be of the type that allows at least moderate employee discretion, or the technology must be altered. In this regard, Electrox made an important decision to reorganize the technology from a functional organization of processes into product-based cells, a strategy that has been shown to be highly conducive to autonomous work groups (Berger, 1994). Many companies, however, fail to make significant changes to technical systems when they are redesigning work (Goodman et al., 1988; Kelly, 1978). In other words, the focus of sociotechnical interventions is usually on changing the "social" systems to fit the "technical" systems rather than jointly changing both of these systems. Indeed, from case studies in a wide range of settings, it has been argued that there is much more potential for influencing the design of technology than is currently exploited (Clegg, Axtell, et al., 1997; Clegg & Ulich, 1987), especially given the spread of new information technologies (Berger, 1994). For example, although often unrecognized, there are choices regarding the allocation of function (i.e., choices regarding what machines do versus what humans do) and the interface between humans and technology (such as the choices involved in the human-computer interface).

Nevertheless, convincing those involved in the design process (usually engineers) to consider such choices is no easy task. As Clegg (1988) has pointed out, psychological and work design issues are traditionally "marginalized" in a "technology-led" design process. Clegg and colleagues have thus made a series of recommendations to counteract this dominant trend (e.g., making users the owners, or project managers, of technical changes, and seeing technologies as supporting "tools"; see Clegg, Waterson, & Carey, 1994).

Systems Within Greenfield Sites

Thus far, we have focused on the alignment of organizational systems that we assume are already in existence. However, what about the case of greenfield sites where such systems are not yet in place? Common sense suggests that the process of introducing enriched work designs will be easier because the opportunity exists to design appropriate human resource and related systems from the outset and because many of the traditional barriers have not yet developed. Certainly, some of the most successful cases of work enrichment have been in plants designed from the start (Emery, 1980; Lawler, 1992).

Nevertheless, although it might seem that the opportunity to design a new plant opens up limitless possibilities, the reality is that "there is no such thing as a truly green field" (Klein, 1994, p. 215). Constraints will exist. Some equipment may already have been purchased, there may be insufficient time to pilot various work design alternatives, and assumptions about the nature of jobs might already be built into budgets and technology. Work design aspects should be considered as early as possible in the planning process, before decisions made about technology and other systems have preempted too many options (Emery, 1980). As a case in point, efforts to involve existing operators in the design of a new plant did not succeed, even though it was nearly 2 years before the planned start-up. This was because operators' recommendations could not be acted on due to high penalty costs imposed by contractors for design modifications.

Considering the Implications
for Multiple Stakeholders

Work redesign is not just a multisystem intervention, as described above, but a change that has implications for multiple parties in the organization. For redesign to be successful, the roles and reactions of many groups of people need to be considered. Reactions can range from overt resistance from those who feel threatened by the work redesign, through apathy from those who perceive it will have little impact on them, to enthusiasm from those who see the potential for personal or organizational benefit. Some of the strongest responses arise because devolving autonomy can change the existing power distribution in the organization (Child, 1984; Clegg, 1984; Cummings, 1978), as shown in Badham, Couchman, and Selden's (1996) account of shop floor work redesign:

> There will be numerous sources of opposition . . . from industrial engineers committed to traditional methods of design and control, from line managers wishing to retain detailed control over production, from trades people opposed to the removal of traditional demarcations and privileges, from union officials perceiving the change as a threat to their power base, from personnel managers reluctant to change pay and classification systems, and from senior managers unwilling to commit resources to a strategic change the benefits of which are not easy to quantify. (p. 341)

We discuss in turn some issues which can surface for the following groups: shop floor employees, support staff, supervisors, managers, and trade union representatives.

Shop Floor Employees

Although we know from research evidence that work redesign typically leads to enhanced job satisfaction, it is a mistake to assume that all employees will welcome the promise of enriched work roles with open arms. Many years of a low-trust culture with a strong "them and us" divide can mean that employees view the changes with suspicion. They may feel that management simply wants them to work harder for no extra pay or that work redesign is a back-door way to cut and eventually abolish overtime or erode demarcation lines. Resistance to the introduction of autonomous work groups also often stems from fears of injustice, such as concerns about pay and the way that decisions will be made (Kirkman et al., 1996).

Given the wide-scale occurrence of downsizing (see Chapter 6), an increasingly common and perhaps more pressing concern of employees is that they will lose their jobs as a result of work redesign. One operator in a steel manufacturing operation, for example, reported that head count in the company had dropped from over 7,500 to 1,500 during his tenure. He commented, "This firm has never spent money on anything without getting rid of jobs." It is easy to see why this operator and many of his peers were fearful about plans to introduce autonomous work groups (Parker et al., 1996). Work redesign should be disentangled from any downsizing programs; otherwise, it will be almost impossible for employees to accept fully the new work roles.

Against this backdrop of uncertainty and suspicion, the promise of more interesting jobs may hold little appeal to many employees, especially if there are no compensating increases in pay. As a consequence of long-term exposure to simplified jobs, aspiration levels may also be low. Employees may have learned, through a process in which taking initiative has been punished or not rewarded, that it is best "not to rock the boat" (Karasek & Theorell, 1990). Indeed, the skills associated with using initiative and taking on responsibility may have been lost. Within Electrox, for instance, supervisors described how hard it was to get operators to make decisions and think for themselves. One commented, "None of the operators knew how to access the computer system, so I said to them 'how do you know which job is a priority?' They said: 'well, its the one on the top of the pile.' They had no idea, and no interest, beyond that" (Parker & Jackson, 1993, p. 46).

Support Staff

Consistent with the sociotechnical systems theory principle that variances should be controlled at the source, work redesign often involves operators taking on tasks that were previously carried out by specialist support staff (e.g., machine setup, routine maintenance, quality inspection). This strategy can result in an eventual reduction in support personnel or, at the very least, substantial changes in their roles. Ways that roles of support staff can be configured when autonomous work groups are introduced (derived from Mohrman & Mohrman, 1997) include

- Support staff as dedicated members of the group
- Support staff as members of multiple groups
- Support staff in shared service groups that provide support to the groups
- Support staff in shared service groups that provide support to the groups as well as training of group members in basic aspects of the skill

On the basis of the principle of grouping together interdependent tasks, the ideal solution often is to have support staff as dedicated team members who report to the same manager, thus creating a fully self-contained autonomous work group. The support staff member can readily train other group members to carry out the support function (or basic aspects of it), and, if the group does not need the support skill full time, the support person can learn other tasks carried out by the group. As well as facilitating training of group members, this option promotes communication between employees and support staff, enhances the support staff person's ownership of a particular area, and allows maximum autonomy for the group.

Nevertheless, although the option of dedicated team membership is preferable in theoretical terms, support staff or specialists often resist integration into teams (Neumann et al., 1995). As illustrated in the example below, they can fear a loss of status, deskilling, and isolation from their functional colleagues. Dedicated membership can also lead to inefficiencies where the workload does not warrant it, and it is clearly inappropriate in cases where there are fewer support staff than there are autonomous work groups. In the latter situation, it would be more appropriate for support staff to be members of multiple groups or for support staff to remain as a separate service group. With both of these options, Mohrman and Morhman (1997) argued it is essential to design in mechanisms that ensure effective coordination and service provision (e.g., contracting or putting in infrastructure to make it easy for specialists to keep up with team activities). Generally, the aim is to move support functions and production closer together, either spatially or in terms of breaking down cultural and psychological barriers (Neumann et al., 1995).

In the case of Electrox, different options were adopted for two groups of support staff that led to different outcomes. Quality inspectors were maintained as a separate service group, but their role changed from inspecting products (which operators were trained to carry out) to auditing processes (i.e., inspecting and improving quality processes and systems). Although initially reluctant, over time the support staff accepted and even preferred their new and more challenging role. However, a different work design was adopted for test engineers who were responsible for electronically testing products. Test engineers were allocated to specific autonomous work groups (which meant that they tested a significantly reduced range of products) and were expected to train other team members to carry out testing while they themselves learned assembly skills. Test engineers strongly resisted this change, and several were so dissatisfied with their loss of status and reduced opportunity to use their fault-finding skills that they left the company. Some of the remaining test engineers, however, eventually found ways to enrich their role, such as by taking on duties devolved by managers.

Supervisors

Insofar as autonomous work groups are introduced, the traditional supervisory role is eliminated because employees carry out the day-to-day supervisory tasks themselves. Those personnel who were supervisors are typically either redeployed into technical or administrative positions (such as coordinating training or marketing), developed into "first-line managers" (see next section), or laid off.

In some cases, however, the supervisory role is maintained, though in a different form (see Table 7.1). One model is that supervisors are retained as group leaders, but their role becomes more strategic and developmental (this is usually reflected in a change of title, such as "facilitator"). However, this has the obvious problem that supervisors can find it hard to devolve responsibility, fearing that they are "giving their job away." Another common model is to introduce team leaders (usually selected from the shop floor) who work "hands on" as part of the team but who are also responsible for coordinating with management and carrying out administrative tasks. A problem that arises with this model is that there is a tendency for the team leader to adopt or recreate the controlling and directing role of a traditional supervisor. Rotating the position of team leader is one way to reduce this tendency.

Given the above implications for roles, it is not surprising that supervisors often resist the introduction of autonomous work groups or other forms of work enrichment (Birchall, 1975; Hackman, 1975; Hackman & Oldham, 1980; Kerr, Hill, & Broedling, 1986). There is also somewhat of a paradox for supervisors in the transition to autonomous work groups. That is, just when they are likely to be experiencing a high degree of uncertainty over their own role, their commitment to facilitating an effective transition is paramount (Parker & Jackson, 1994). Within Electrox, a subset of the supervisors became first-line managers (the remainder were redeployed into backup positions) and, as such, were expected to adopt a new style of leadership. This change required much persistence on the part of the new first-line managers. One told how he had to resist the temptation to tell people what to do and instead had to coach them to think for themselves. For instance, when an employee asked how she could improve her appraisal score, the manager told her that she needed to take more initiative and gave some examples of the sorts of things she could do. The employee then went and carried out all of the tasks suggested by the supervisor. She then came back to the manager and said, "I've done all that you suggested; what shall I do next?" It was only after much support and coaching from the manager that the employee came to understand the true meaning of initiative. This example illustrates the difficulty of the new leadership role and

TABLE 7.1 Different Options for Leadership of Autonomous Work Groups

Model	Advantages	Problems/Concerns
Group carries out supervisory tasks by itself and is led by a first-line manager (who may supervise two or more other groups).	This is the approach most consistent with the work design principles outlined in Chapter 4. These work groups tend to have the highest degree of self-management and therefore are likely to reap the greatest benefits.	Group can experience problems with group decision making (conflict, etc.). One or more "natural leaders" can emerge, causing conflict among members. The lack of a single contact point can cause problems for people outside the group. Existing supervisors often feel threatened. Transition to "first-line manager" can be difficult.
Group has a "hands-on" team leader (rather than a supervisor) who reports directly to a manager.	Team leaders have knowledge of technical and social aspects of the organization. They typically know the personalities and skill base of the group, and are often more likely to be trusted. The move toward completely self-managing teams is often too threatening and radical for companies, so this represents a "safer" option.	Team leaders can be no more than "cheap" supervisors. It can be difficult for team leaders to establish their role (e.g., they can feel unsure as to whose "side" they are on and can find it hard to establish authority). Team leaders can lack the necessary interpersonal or technical skills needed to coordinate the group. Those who were previously "supervisors" often feel threatened.

TABLE 7.1 Continued

Model	Advantages	Problems/Concerns
Group retains the existing supervisor as its leader, but the supervisor adopts a new role (empowering, etc.).	There is greater continuity, with existing relations between supervisors and operators maintained. The supervisor is usually technically skilled and familiar with people. The supervisor is in a key position to act as a change agent because he or she relates to managers and the shop floor. This model avoids problems with supervisory unions.	Supervisors often maintain a controlling and directing style, finding it difficult to "let go" (because they fear loss of control, status, or even their job or because they lack the skills), thus inhibiting employee autonomy. Supervisors often lack the necessary interpersonal skills that are required (e.g., a coaching style).

NOTE: These are not the only options (e.g., some groups have team leaders and supervisors).

at the same time shows the importance of the manager (i.e., the ex-supervisor) as a key change agent.

Ideally, no matter which option for leadership is chosen, supervisors should be assured that even if the traditional supervisory role becomes redundant, they will not be. They should be given the opportunity to develop skills appropriate to their new role (Grey & Corlett, 1989; Parker & Jackson, 1994; see Alasoini, 1996, for some case examples of successful transitions). Moreover, all those involved (managers, supervisors, and employees) also need a clear and shared understanding of the new leadership role (Walton, 1985).

Managers

As described above, the introduction of autonomous work groups often involves eliminating supervisors as a level between shop floor employees and managers. First-line managers usually have a wider span of control than supervisors (e.g., they may be responsible for managing two or more groups), and their role is strategic and human resource oriented rather than directing and controlling (Child & Partridge, 1982). For example, the first-line manager is expected to set the broad objectives for the team (Cordery & Wall, 1985), facilitate employee development so that employees can function autonomously (Parker & Jackson, 1994), and ensure that the team has sufficient knowledge, skills, information, authority, and resources to perform effectively (Lawler, 1986, 1992). Cordery (1996) described the requirements as follows: "considerate, participative supervision, an absence of close monitoring, along with effective boundary management" (p. 239).

More generally, encouraging and retraining managers within an organization to "empower" employees is an indirect way of bringing about work redesign. Neumann et al. (1995) identified three types of changes that are necessary for the development of a new management style: *a change in role* (e.g., a movement away from a "hands-on," "fire-fighting" type of role to a more strategic, planning type of role), *a change in attitudes and behaviors* (toward an interpersonal, coaching style), and *a change in expectations* (e.g., the removal of external symbols of management status, such as cars or styles of clothing).

A further way in which management roles are affected by work redesign concerns the alignment of organizational systems and structures described earlier (e.g., reward, control systems). Within Electrox, for example, it was necessary to consider changing the management structure to align indirect functions with the autonomous work groups that they supported (Parker & Jackson, 1994). Quality personnel and maintenance engineers often experienced conflicting priorities because, although working as an integral part of production, they were accountable to a quality and engineering manager, respectively. Unfortunately, although the need to change reporting structures was obvious, management resistance proved to be a major stumbling block.

Difficulties with senior levels of management can relate to a lack of interest in work design to begin with, or "organizational inertia." Traditionally, many managers have been reluctant to improve working practices for reasons of health, safety, or quality of work life unless they are convinced that there will be an adequate return on the investment or unless they are forced to do so through legislation (Asplund, 1981). However, with the current economic imperative for more flexible forms of work organization (as described in Chapters 5 and 6), senior management these days is more likely to consider work redesign. The problem instead is that these managers often do not fully understand the scope of the change that is required, and their interest can pale when they realize the implications of work redesign for the wider organization. Yet, as with all forms of organizational change, full support and commitment is needed from the highest level (Pearce & Ravlin, 1987; Tannenbaum, Salas, & Cannon-Bowers, 1996; see also Chapter 8).

Trade Unions

Many trade unions welcome work enrichment, seeing it as essential for the company's survival and as consistent with a long-term goal of increasing employee participation in decision making (Ephlin, 1988). Other trade unions, however, fear the implications of work redesign for their members or even their own power base. For example, when Volkswagen formed semiautonomous work groups at Salzgitter in 1975, the unions saw informally elected work group leaders as potentially threatening their power (Littler & Salaman, 1985).

Some trade unions resist work redesign because they are concerned that they will lose members through the removal of demarcation lines (usually necessary for multiskilling) and because they fear that decreased membership will erode their size and strength. Some believe that work redesign will have no effect on the distribution of power at all and that it is actually a means of extracting cooperation from employees while maintaining control over them (Kelly, 1982). In other words, work redesign can be seen as a back-door way to change pay and work conditions, increase employee workload, obtain cheaper supervisors, pit individual employees against each other, or weaken the traditional importance of seniority (Buchanan & McCalman, 1989; Parker & Slaughter, 1988). An example of such resistance is the

Union of Communication Workers in Britain, who in 1992 voted to oppose the introduction of team working in Royal Mail.

In summary, work design is inevitably embedded within a wider organization context. Human resource, control and information, and technological systems need to be aligned with the work design for changes in roles to be sustained, and the implications for multiple stakeholders need to be considered from the outset. If the redesign of work is attempted without consideration of these broader issues, it does so at the risk of failure and small or temporary change. Work redesign is thus not a simple case of choosing from a range of "off-the-shelf" packages; rather, it is a process that needs careful management. We turn in the next chapter to investigate some of the ways of managing this process: that is, the mechanics of actually redesigning work.

8

Redesigning Work (Part 2): Managing the Change Process

W ork redesign can be achieved in multiple ways. It can be a deliberate and structured change initiative, it can be brought in on the back of the introduction of various modern initiatives (such as total quality management), or it can be part of a long-term organizational and cultural change involving the gradual removal of rigid demarcation lines, the abolition of piecework, and the introduction of training programs to encourage managers to devolve decision-making power. Correspondingly, the particular mechanics and methods of achieving new work roles will differ.

In all cases, however, the way the change is introduced will be central to success. As Tannenbaum et al. (1996) observed, "The process of change is likely to be as important as the shape of the new structure" (p. 523). The process of redesigning work is our focus in the present chapter. First, we highlight the importance of employee participation in the change process. Assuming participation as an underlying component, we then suggest eight key phases involved in structured work redesign. Finally, we describe some useful tools and methods to facilitate the redesign process, and we highlight the fundamental role of a change agent.

The Principle of Participation

The message here is a simple one: involve people who will be affected by the work redesign in its planning and implementation (Davis & Wacker, 1987; Mohrman & Mohrman, 1997). Such an approach is specified in the sociotechnical systems principle of compatibility: That is, if the objectives of work redesign are to create a system capable of adapting to change and using the creative capacities of people, then the design process should reflect this (Cherns, 1976, 1987).

The usual approach is to involve representatives from all stakeholder groups (such as line managers, supervisors, operators, trade union officials, support staff, and human resource personnel). Not only is the end solution likely to be a high-quality one because many different perspectives are brought to bear on the issue, but there is a greater chance of acceptance and ownership of the work redesign from all concerned. Shop floor employees in particular need to identify with the new design and want it to work, as well as to understand the rationale behind the design, so as to anticipate and minimize any potential negative effects (Davis & Wacker, 1987). This principle of participation extends to the design and implementation of new technologies and techniques, processes that are traditionally handled by technical specialists (such as engineers) and production managers (Berger, 1994; Clegg, Coleman, et al., 1996).

Although managing the process of participation is not easy (as this chapter will show), it is widely accepted that involving people is important for work redesign as well as other forms of organizational change (Locke & Schweiger, 1979). In a simulation study, Seeborg (1978) showed how jobs redesigned by subjects for themselves had positive effects on their reactions, whereas the exact same changes imposed on subjects by others had a much less positive impact. Similarly, Parker et al. (1995) reported positive effects of just-in-time practices on work characteristics when employees participated in the change process but negative consequences when they did not.

Phases in Structured
Work Redesign

We recommend eight broad phases (summarized in Figure 8.1) for structured work redesign projects within production settings (also applicable to routine office work settings). Our intention is not to be prescriptive but to make the reader aware of the sorts of activities that will be required. We assume that it has already been decided that work redesign fits with the goals of the organization.

Phase 1: Set the Direction

Because there are a myriad of ways in which work redesign can proceed, it is necessary to "set the direction" and agree on the parameters and objectives of the project. This includes clarifying

- The specific aims (what the project is intended to achieve)
- The scope (which departments will be involved and which roles will be affected). In deciding where to focus, identify circumstances where there is a strong chance of success, the potential for a large impact, a chance to address problems at their source, the possibility to link in with other organizational developments, and support from stakeholders (Kompier, 1996).
- The key change roles (who will be responsible for driving the change)
- The approach to design and implementation (whether there will be a steering committee, how much discretion the change agent has, etc.)
- The composition of the design team (who the stakeholders are, etc.)

(Note that some of these decisions might have to be made after Phases 2 and 3).

From the outset, it is critical that the design team have support and strategic input from senior management. The latter need to make it clear what outcomes they expect from the work redesign, and they need to be prepared to invest sufficient resources (time, effort, money, support, etc.) into the change process. Inevitably, there will be some strategic decisions that the design team does not have the information, authority, or impartiality to make (such as those involving payment systems, layoffs, or demarcations). Senior management will need to take a lead in such decisions, though with input from the team. Ultimately, the design team needs to know what it is aiming for and to understand what constraints it is working within, yet at the same time it must have sufficient autonomy to be creative.

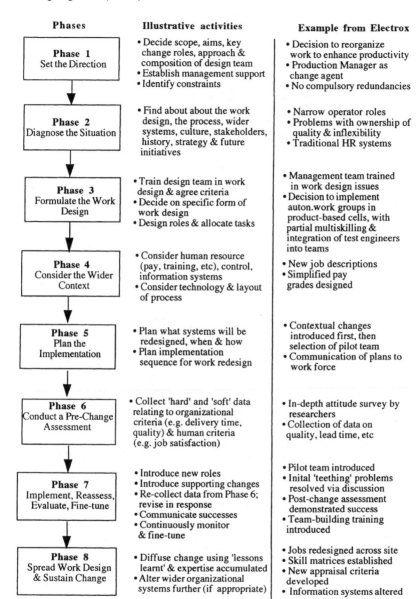

Phases	Illustrative activities	Example from Electrox
Phase 1 Set the Direction	• Decide scope, aims, key change roles, approach & composition of design team • Establish management support • Identify constraints	• Decision to reorganize work to enhance productivity • Production Manager as change agent • No compulsory redundancies
Phase 2 Diagnose the Situation	• Find about about the work design, the process, wider systems, culture, stakeholders, history, strategy & future initiatives	• Narrow operator roles • Problems with ownership of quality & inflexibility • Traditional HR systems
Phase 3 Formulate the Work Design	• Train design team in work design & agree criteria • Decide on specific form of work design • Design roles & allocate tasks	• Management team trained in work design issues • Decision to implement auton.work groups in product-based cells, with partial multiskilling & integration of test engineers into teams
Phase 4 Consider the Wider Context	• Consider human resource (pay, training, etc), control, information systems • Consider technology & layout of process	• New job descriptions • Simplified pay grades designed
Phase 5 Plan the Implementation	• Plan what systems will be redesigned, when & how • Plan implementation sequence for work redesign	• Contextual changes introduced first, then selection of pilot team • Communication of plans to work force
Phase 6 Conduct a Pre-Change Assessment	• Collect 'hard' and 'soft' data relating to organizational criteria (e.g. delivery time, quality) & human criteria (e.g. job satisfaction)	• In-depth attitude survey by researchers • Collection of data on quality, lead time, etc
Phase 7 Implement, Reassess, Evaluate, Fine-tune	• Introduce new roles • Introduce supporting changes • Re-collect data from Phase 6; revise in response • Communicate successes • Continuously monitor & fine-tune	• Pilot team introduced • Inital 'teething' problems resolved via discussion • Post-change assessment demonstrated success • Team-building training introduced
Phase 8 Spread Work Design & Sustain Change	• Diffuse change using 'lessons learnt' & expertise accumulated • Alter wider organizational systems further (if appropriate)	• Jobs redesigned across site • Skill matrices established • New appraisal criteria developed • Information systems altered

Figure 8.1. Key Phases in Structured Work Redesign

Phase 2: Diagnose the Situation

An "information-gathering" phase is necessary to help identify what form of work redesign is appropriate or feasible, as well as how the implementation process might proceed. Aspects to find out about include

- The existing work design (key tasks, who makes what decisions, etc.)
- The production process (work flow, non-value-added activities, etc.)
- Wider organizational structure and systems (i.e., human resources, control, and information systems, technology)
- Cultural aspects (management style, etc.)
- Who the key stakeholders are, and their views regarding relevant issues
- Salient historical events (such as previous efforts to redesign work)
- Planned initiatives or emerging changes that might affect work roles
- Strategic aspects that might affect work design choices (company goals, market changes, requirements for competitiveness, future technological advances, etc.)

No single technique can provide data on all of these aspects, and a range of methods should be used, such as attitude surveys, collecting objective data (e.g., absence levels and performance), observations, interviews, focus group discussion, tracer studies (in which a product is studied as it goes through the process), and benchmarking against other companies. Involving the design team in the diagnosis phase not only equips team members with the necessary understanding but facilitates their developing a shared sense that work redesign is the way to address organizational problems (Beer, Eisenstat, & Spector, 1990) and helps create a sense of procedural justice in the process (Kirkman et al., 1996).

Phase 3: Formulate an Appropriate Work Design

Design team members need initially to develop a shared understanding about what an "appropriate work design" involves. To this end, team members will need some training in basic work design concepts. The principles and criteria described in Chapter 2 provide a starting point (see also Table 8.1), and the team can generate additional criteria (e.g., "A good work design will be one that reduces levels of scrap"). To broaden team members' horizons regarding work design possibilities, it can be useful to visit other departments or organizations to see different models. Training in problem-solving methods is also useful because it gives the design team a shared language and set of skills (Alasoini, 1996).

TABLE 8.1 Critical Work Design Decisions

Design Decision	Recommendations
Individual or group work design?	Where jobs are interdependent, choose a group form of work design.
Where will the boundary of the job/team be?	Aim to create a job, or team, that is as self-contained as possible (i.e., that contains interdependencies). Where all the interdependencies cannot be contained within the group, design integrating mechanisms.
How autonomous/ self-managing should the team be?	Allow the team to perform as many management tasks as possible, especially if the production environment is uncertain. However, recognize that self-management is a developmental process, and ensure that team members are given the appropriate training and information to support the high autonomy.
How will the team be run?	Ideally, allow teams to run themselves with strategic input from "first-line managers." Note that in the context of complex knowledge work where information-processing requirements are excessive, Mohrman et al. (1995) suggested that a designated leader will be needed to coordinate the group.
What is the role of support staff?	Ideally, have support staff as dedicated team members (although this is not always practical; see Chapter 8, the section "Support Staff").
What degree and type of multiskilling are best?	Partial multiskilling is often best because it allows for cover, provides flexibility, and enables sharing of undesirable tasks, yet limits training costs and reduces the likelihood of employees' forgetting skills they have learned (see Cross, 1986, and Cordery, 1996).
How will employees be allocated to groups?	If possible, take the opportunity to create groups with an appropriate mix of skills and personalities, rather than just relying on existing groups of people.
What mechanisms should be put in place to ensure that teams cooperate with other individuals or teams?	Put in place formal and informal mechanisms to ensure that team members communicate with relevant others outside the group (e.g., identify liaison roles and create teams with overlapping memberships; Mohrman & Mohrman, 1997).

Once team members have a shared understanding of work design criteria, the design process can begin. Table 8.1 summarizes some of the key decisions that need to be made. Various methods and tools can be used in this phase, as discussed later in this chapter.

Phase 4: Consider the Wider Context

As discussed in Chapter 7, modifications to organizational systems will probably be necessary. The layout may also need to be reconfigured. Consider the following requirements:

- Flexible and broad job/role descriptions
- Reward/grading systems that promote appropriate behaviors
- Systems to monitor and facilitate training
- Nonhierarchical career paths
- Recruitment and selection systems based on appropriate criteria
- Control systems that facilitate employee discretion
- Clear performance criteria/clear targets or objectives (negotiated by the group or individual)
- Information/feedback systems that allow employees to act on problems that arise, make appropriate decisions, interact effectively with other groups, and learn from their mistakes
- Layout of work environment conducive to the redesign (e.g., team members near each other and in an area separate from other teams)
- Modifications to technology to support enriched work roles

Phase 5: Plan the Implementation

Having identified what forms of work design and supporting systems are appropriate, the next step is to plan how these will be implemented. In many cases, it will not be feasible or appropriate to adapt all of the contextual systems before work redesign (Beer et al., 1990; Morhman et al., 1995). Some changes may be more than the company is prepared to support, some will emerge as important only with the learning that occurs after implementation, and some (such as team-based reward systems) can only work when the redesign is in place. Mohrman et al. (1995) recommended asking, "Given that all aspects of the design cannot be put in place at once, where should we start?" (p. 31).

The importance of this phase is illustrated by the experiences of a wire-making company (Sprigg et al., 1996). Eighteen months were spent planning for the implementation of self-managing teams, including the following: negotiating with the unions to remove demarcations, changing pay and work conditions to align with team working, carefully selecting and training team leaders, and communicating the plans for team working to the workforce. When teams were introduced, key stakeholders agreed that the implementation proceeded remarkably smoothly.

An operator commented, "To be honest, I'm amazed at how well team working has gone in."

Phase 6: Conduct a Pre-Change Assessment

Pre-change assessment, including collecting "soft" data (e.g., employee opinions) and "hard" data (e.g., performance records, customer satisfaction), is important for two reasons. First, it provides diagnostic information (see Phase 2). Second, it serves as a baseline against which the subsequent effects of the change can be compared. Systematic evaluation is needed to counter bias, both positive and negative, that can otherwise lead to inappropriate conclusions about the work redesign (Hackman, 1975).

Evaluation is particularly key for those employees involved in the work redesign who can otherwise lose sight of where they started from. New dissatisfactions with the redesigned work need to be weighed against past dissatisfactions. For example, after a pilot autonomous work group had been introduced within Electrox, managers became concerned about negative comments made by team members. However, through our independent investigation, we were able to show that levels of employee job satisfaction (which were already higher than norms) remained high after the work redesign, even despite considerably raised expectations. When we asked members of the pilot team whether they would like to return to their old way of working, the response was overwhelmingly "no" (Parker & Jackson, 1994).

Phase 7: Implement, Reassess, Evaluate, and Fine-Tune

Implementation should be considered as an evolving process that requires considerable learning and adjustment (Mohrman, et al., 1995). Decisions about who does which particular tasks, for example, are likely to be revised in the light of feedback from group members, and levels of autonomy can increase over time as skills develop. Cherns (1987) referred to this in terms of the "Incompletion or Forth Bridge Principle," reflecting the fact that the painting of the Forth Bridge is no sooner finished than it needs to start again. The redesign process should therefore be one that involves continual assessment (including repeating Phase 6) and fine-tuning. Those involved in the work design process should expect to have to revise and reformulate as the work design evolves and changes in response to external and internal pressures. Successes should be widely communicated, and areas identified for improvement should be acted on.

Phase 8: Spread the Work Redesign and Sustain the Change

In cases in which a pilot approach has been taken, the intention will be to spread the work redesign throughout the organization. This can be facilitated by using the expertise that has developed (such as by moving into the new areas those individuals who were involved in setting up the initiative or those employees who have successfully made the transition) and by drawing on "lessons learned."

Nevertheless, it is also likely that the wider spread of work redesign will require more substantial changes to organizational systems and structures. In Electrox, the pilot initiative succeeded without including a test engineer in the team because there was already so much technical support for the group. Yet this could not be a template for the wider introduction of autonomous work groups because of the plan to integrate test engineers into the teams. Thus, despite the successful pilot initiative, difficult issues involving test engineers' resistance still had to be addressed.

Sustainable change cannot be brought about in an instant. In Mohrman et al.'s (1995) terms, the introduction of new forms of work organization will not be achieved by a "one shot implementation" (p. 31) but will be a gradual transition that takes many years and much learning.

Methods and Tools to Support Work Redesign

There are various useful methods and tools to support the above process of work design (particularly applicable to Phase 3, formulating an appropriate work design).

Identifying Tasks and Processes

Work redesign initiatives typically involve identifying the key tasks performed by the workforce and the key processes. Methods used to identify the key tasks range from *brainstorming* what the key the tasks are, to using more sophisticated methods of *job analysis* (see Spector, Brannick, & Coovert, 1989). A range of methods can be used to identify the key work processes, such as *tracer studies* (in which a product is studied as it proceeds through the work flow), *process simulation games* (in which the production process is simulated by those who perform it; e.g., Hakamaki & Forssen-Nyberg, 1996), *transformation flowcharts* (in which the key transformations to the product are identified; Davis & Wacker,

1987), and *process mapping* (in which the processes and how they evolve over time are mapped, along with the general skill sets that are required; Mohrman & Mohrman, 1997).

Combining Tasks

Methods are then needed to work out how to combine the key tasks into jobs or into groups. Davis and Wacker (1987) suggested simply *rating the tasks according to work design criteria* and then using these ratings to group tasks so that each job or team has a balance of desirable or undesirable tasks, isolated and collaborative work, simple and complex tasks, and so on. Other methods, such as the *task interdependence analysis* described by Mohrman et al. (1995), focus more explicitly on grouping interlinked tasks. The latter analysis (which goes hand in hand with process mapping) involves identifying what interdependencies exist between processes, the nature of these interdependencies (e.g., routine or complex, reciprocal or one-way), and the best ways of dealing with these interdependencies (e.g., routine interdependencies can be handled by specifications or procedures, whereas complex and reciprocal interdependencies should be built into the team).

A related method, derived from sociotechnical systems theory, is that of *variance analysis* (see Davis & Wacker, 1987, for details and Wall, Corbett, Martin, et al., 1990, for an illustration). A simplified version of variance analysis involves the following steps:

1. List all variances, or deviations from planned operations, that affect the process (e.g., poor quality supplies, breakdowns, changes in product design).
2. Identify key variances because a large percentage of problems are usually caused by a small percentage of variances (a key variance is one that can have serious consequences, interacts with other variances, cannot be predicted with certainty, and can be controlled by timely human action).
3. Draft a table of key variance control that shows how, where, and by whom each key variance can be detected, corrected, and prevented.
4. Construct a table of the skills, knowledge, information, and authority needed for employees to be able to control key variances (see Table 8.2 for some illustrative output).
5. Create new jobs so that as many key variances as possible can be controlled by jobholders themselves.

More sophisticated approaches to grouping tasks are described elsewhere (e.g., Clegg, Coleman, et al., 1996).

TABLE 8.2   Skills, Knowledge, Information, and Authority
Needed to Control Key Variances

Key Variance to Be Controlled	Skills/Knowledge Needed	Information Needed	Local Authority Needed
Machine stoppage due to worn Part X	Able to recognize the problem (diagnostic skills) plus basic mechanical skills to replace Part X	Machine operating procedures; information about supply of Part X.	Authority to acquire and replace Part X (i.e., maintenance do not have to be involved)
Problem with quality of steel supplied	Ability to diagnose the problem; ability to talk to supplier	Quality standards (tolerances) for steel; supplier contact details	Authority to stop production and to contact supplier directly

SOURCE: Adapted from "Job Design," by L. E. Davis & G. J. Wacker, 1987, in G. Salvendy (Ed.), *Handbook of Human Factors*, New York: John Wiley. Copyright John Wiley & Sons Limited. Reproduced with permission.

Comparing Work Design Options

Whatever method is used to make decisions about how to combine tasks into jobs or teams, it is clear that there will typically not be a single solution but rather a range of work design options. A method that explicitly involves identifying these options and then evaluating their costs and benefits is the *scenarios method* (Clegg, Coleman, et al., 1996). This approach is particularly useful when identifying different ways to configure work designs for new systems or technologies. Many tools also exist to facilitate the inclusion of human and organizational factors into the design and implementation of new technological systems (Clegg, Coleman, et al., 1996; Lim, Long, & Silcock, 1992; Mumford, 1986).

Clarifying Roles and Responsibilities

To determine and clarify "who does what" within a work setting, a useful tool is the *responsibility chart* (Melcher, 1967; see Table 8.3 for an illustration). Responsibility charting involves identifying who is responsible for what key tasks.

The chart format can also be used to delineate decision-making responsibilities. The key parties potentially involved in the decision are listed down one side, and the key decisions are listed along the top. The role of each party in the decision is then shown, using a key such as that described by Morhman et al. (1995):

TABLE 8.3 An Illustrative Responsibility Chart for a Self-Managing Team

	Team Now	*Team in 6 Months*	*Manager*
Arrange breaks	X		
Monitor quality standards	X		
Allocate tasks		X	
Order raw materials		X	
Develop and monitor training plans		X	X
Liaise with other teams		X	X
Liaise with senior management			X
Identify team objectives		X	X
Handle disciplinary problems			X
Decide and allocate budget		X	X

D: the authority to decide
R: the authority to recommend
I: the authority to provide input
N: the need to know
U: no involvement (p. 189)

The decision-making chart can include an escalation path that shows the path to be followed if the first group with authority cannot come to agreement (e.g., if a team cannot make a decision, team members might escalate the decision to the first-line manager). These and other charting methods are clearly useful in clarifying roles and responsibilities, but note that the charts should be revised over time as the group becomes more self-managing.

Mapping Skills

Skills matrices are useful for identifying where there are gaps in skill coverage, for planning training needs, and for monitoring skill development. Skill matrices typically have the job incumbents listed across the top and the skills/training requirements listed down the side. Various symbols are then used to depict the situation, such as the following:

O   Basic awareness
●   Basic skills (requires supervision)
☐   Competent (can carry out task on own)
■   Fully competent (able to train others)

This general matrix structure can be adapted for other purposes, such as to indicate training plans or to show interactions between people.

Adapting Technically Oriented Methods

Tools to redesign work can be derived from various *technically oriented methods*. There is an abundance of problem-solving and analytic tools (such as quality improvement techniques) that can be modified to focus on work design aspects or that can be used "as they are" but with the explicit inclusion of work design criteria. For example, fishbone diagrams can be used to identify the major causes of nonproductive time (such as scheduling problems or breakdowns), and employees can then brainstorm ways to address these problems, with explicit encouragement from the change agent to consider nontechnical solutions (Alasoini, 1996, described a specific method using this approach). Using tools in this way is consistent with Goodman et al.'s (1988) recommendation to improve group performance by identifying the main productivity levers in a technological system and then focusing on those areas where human and organizational factors can make the biggest difference.

An Effective Change Agent

A highly skilled facilitator, or "change agent," is usually needed to facilitate the complex human dynamics that are involved in work redesign. The change agent can be someone internal, with the obvious advantage being that this person would know the organizational context. However, there are several benefits of an external change agent. Compared with an internal candidate, an external person will have a wider perspective, be less constrained by organizational norms and values, be less biased toward particular groups, and be better able to integrate multiple perspectives.

If an external agent is brought in, a particular type is needed. We believe that, given that there is no "one best way" for work design, the change agent role is best performed by someone using process facilitation skills (Schein, 1969) and/or action research skills (see, e.g., Kemp et al., 1980) rather than by an "expert" consultant who "tells people what to do." Davis and Wacker (1987) similarly argued that the change agent should aim, not to design the job, but to guide others in this process. They identified the following as key roles:

- Training and guidance on work design principles and methods
- Process facilitation (e.g., planning, clarifying, asking questions, giving feedback)
- Mediating (e.g., acting as a neutral broker)
- Research
- Spreading the ideas to other parts of the institution

One way of thinking about the role of a work design change agent is as performing a "polyfiller" role (e.g., Badham et al., 1996). That is, at various stages, the change agent is involved in lobbying for action, providing training, and a range of other activities to prevent "breakdown" or "lags" in the change process. Because work redesign can raise fundamental issues about control, this can be a highly political process (Badham et al., 1996; Emery, 1980; Kemp et al., 1980; Whybrow & Parker, 1997).

A critical yet difficult role for the change agent concerns effective facilitation of the participative process. The quote below vividly shows that effective facilitation requires a high level of interpersonal skill and is much more than mastery of a particular method or tool:

> A method cannot reveal the fact that someone in the room has just realized his/her job will no longer be the same in the future and has started to panic. It cannot manage reactions of people who are distressed because they discover that their work, to which they are strongly identified, does not add value to the process being studied. Nor can it feel that people in the group are not expressing their ideas because they do not dare to propose something that will change the social status of their peers. . . . The method itself does not motivate the right people or convince them to contribute their expertise at the right time. It cannot distinguish when people are voicing resistance to change or bringing real arguments to adapt the project in the light of workers' experience. (Blatti, 1996, p. 402)

Managing the process of participation requires the change agent to operate at both cognitive and emotive levels. Regarding the former, participants often have "tunnel vision" in relation to work design possibilities, and suggestions that they make will be influenced by their past experiences and their expectations for the future. Davis and Wacker (1987), for instance, described how employees involved in redesigning their work saw their needs as being met by getting a second time clock so that they would not lose time clocking out for lunch. Their experience inhibited them from realizing that work redesign can address more fundamental issues. Part of the design process should therefore be educational: that is, aimed at broadening people's frames of reference in relation to work design possibilities.

Emotions (such as fear, anger, and feeling under threat) will arise during the participation process and need to be managed. In this respect, Klein (1994) discussed the value of "transitional systems" in facilitating change, such as process simulation games, role plays, and so on—the important point being that the method or process should create a "safe" environment in which "people can experiment with roles and behaviours beyond their habitual ones, and where issues can be worked through that the normal working culture may not allow to surface" (p. 218).

Unanswered Questions

In the previous two chapters, we described the process of work redesign as a complex one but as one that can nevertheless be successful if attention is given to wider organizational systems, the roles of multiple stakeholders, and the sequence of participative phases that are typically involved.

Nevertheless, there is still much that we do not know about how to introduce work redesign successfully. In 1980, Oldham and Hackman raised more than 50 research questions regarding the process of work redesign, ranging from specific issues (such as "What are the consequences of changing job descriptions alone?") to general ones (such as "What factors cause work design plans to fail to be implemented?"). Unfortunately, as we have discovered while writing these chapters, there has been remarkably little progress in this domain (see also Oldham, 1996). We need systematic studies that ask, for example: Which methods of work redesign work and which don't? What are the risks and benefits of alternative work design strategies? How can the participation process best be facilitated? How does one redesign roles within the constraints imposed by new systems such as just-in-time? How can we design and install new technologies in a way that better accommodates work design principles? The list of important questions to address is endless. However, as we reflect on in our final chapter, it is unlikely that these will ever be adequately addressed if we continue carrying out research in the same way as the bulk of the published literature. A more flexible and pluralistic approach (e.g., encompassing qualitative studies) is needed.

9

Conclusions

We set out in this book to map existing knowledge on how work design choices affect employee attitudes and behavior and, at the same time, to identify the key issues for research in the future. What, then, are the primary messages in these respects?

The first point to make is that there are indeed choices for work design. It is too often taken for granted that designing simplified jobs is the only option. However, there are clearly alternatives, and we encourage managers, engineers, and all those who are traditionally involved in designing jobs to consider the full range of job design possibilities. To this end, we strongly advocate involving employees whose jobs will be affected in the process of choosing, developing, and implementing an appropriate work design.

Second, there is strong and consistent evidence that some form of enriched work design will be the best option for most employees. Studies across many contexts show that redesigning work to increase the variety of tasks (job enlargement), but especially to enhance employees' autonomy and decision-making authority (job enrichment/autonomous work groups), will promote better mental health and increase job satisfaction among employees. Work redesign therefore provides a vehicle by which to minimize or even prevent stress in the workplace—the importance of which should not be underestimated in the light of an ever-more-demanding modern workplace. Thus, leaving aside for the moment the productivity-related consequences of a dissatisfied or stressed workforce (such as the costs associated with increased absence, turnover, and litigation), there is a clear *human* imperative to enrich work.

Some countries have taken this research evidence sufficiently seriously to introduce legislation regarding the design of work. In Sweden's amended Work Environment Act, for example, Section 1 states, "The employee shall be given the opportunity to participate in designing his own working situation and in processes of change and development affecting his work" (cited in Kompier, 1996, p. 359). Holland has recently introduced similar legislation. We believe that such government policy serves to counterbalance the narrow commercial emphasis that organizations typically have. Indeed, this is the whole purpose of social policy. As Lafitte (1962) stated,

> Through collective action, particularly by imposing the state's directing power on the forces of the market, we seek to steer society along paths it would not naturally follow. . . . Through social policy, we assert the primacy of non-economic values, our belief that the way of life matters more than the ways of getting a living. (p. 58)

A third key message is that although evidence regarding whether work redesign promotes better employee performance is mixed, it is nevertheless sufficient to warrant continued investigation. An especially fruitful approach will be to identify those circumstances in which work redesign is most likely to promote better performance, such as the importance of interdependence for autonomous group working and the greater potential learning gains that can accrue from work enrichment within highly uncertain production contexts.

Identifying contingencies that affect the extent to which work redesign promotes performance is one way that work design theory should be expanded, and in Chapters 3 and 4 we suggested several other ways (such as the need to consider a broader range of work characteristics and outcome variables and to investigate mechanisms). We argued that an expanded theoretical approach will help us better to understand how modern technologies and developments (such as just-in-time, teleworking, and downsizing) affect the nature of work and, at the same time, will enable us to identify proactively the forms of work design that are most appropriate for modern organizations (e.g., that allow best use of new technology). The changing workplace has thus brought many research questions to the surface, questions that will be best addressed by a broader theoretical approach than that taken hitherto.

This brings us to a fourth key point. To influence work design practice to a greater extent than is now the case, we need to know much more about *how* to redesign jobs successfully. In other words, when we recommend enriching work, we will be in a stronger position if we can simultaneously give clear and empirically derived advice about the most effective ways to manage the process. As we pointed out in Chapter 8, research in this area is lagging behind. To this end, we suggest (along with others, e.g., Clegg, Waterson, & Axtell, 1996) the greater use of qualitative approaches to allow a better understanding of the complex, and often highly political, dynamics that are involved in work redesign. We also advocate the wider reporting of "process issues" (in most published work design studies, the focus is on outcomes rather than process). In addition, there is a need for further development of research-based tools, implementation guidelines, and design principles to assist organizations in proactively redesigning work on the basis of criteria other than those of simplification. Because work redesign interventions are rarely anything other than multisystem interventions that involve multiple stakeholders, we would like to see the growth of theories that reflect this complexity. Such theoretical development will benefit from the integration of perspectives and research from disciplines other than psychology (such as sociology, anthropology, engineering, and management), as well as the integration of international perspectives and ideas. Regarding the latter point, there has been a tendency for North American research to proceed somewhat independently of theoretical development within Europe.

As never before, the time is ripe to develop our understanding of work redesign. The increasing prevalence of "empowerment," "team working," and other such initiatives shows that there has been a definite swing toward enriching jobs. Indeed, this is a trend that is not just reported in the literature but observable in our day-to-day contact with organizations. Nowadays, when we go into companies advocating greater employee autonomy, our voices are heard (our recommendations are sometimes even acted on!). But although we welcome this greater interest in work design, we also foresee a danger. That is, if organizations attempt to redesign work but do so inappropriately (e.g., without making the necessary cultural and organizational changes), then the work redesign is unlikely to be successful. Work enrichment could become seen as just another "management fad" rather than the substantive initiative, grounded in a long tradition of research, that it is. We hope that this book, in describing where work design has come from and showing where it can potentially take us, will keep work design on the agenda.

References

Abernathy, W., Clark, K., & Kantrow, A. (1981). The new industrial competition. *Harvard Business Review, 59,* 51-68.

Adams, J. S. (1965). Inequity in social exchange. In L. Berkowitz (Ed.), *Advances in experimental social psychology* (Vol. 2, pp. 267-299). New York: Academic Press.

Adler, N. J. (1984). Women do not want international careers: And other myths about international management. *Organizational Dynamics, 13,* 66-79.

Adler, P. S., & Borys, B. (1989). Automation and skill: Three generations of research on the NC case. *Politics and Society, 17,* 377-402.

Aeillo, J. R. (1993). Computer-based work monitoring: Electronic surveillance and its effects. *Journal of Applied Social Psychology, 23,* 499-507.

Alasoini, T. (1996). A learning factory: Experimenting with adaptable production in Finnish engineering workshops. *International Journal of Human Factors in Manufacturing, 6,* 3-19.

Alban-Metcalfe, B. M., & Nicholson, N. (1984). *The career development of British managers.* London: British Institute of Management Foundation.

Aldag, R. J., & Brief, A. P. (1979). *Task design and employee motivation.* Glenview, IL: Scott, Foresman.

Algera, J. A. (1983). "Objective" and perceived task characteristics as a determinant of reactions by task performers. *Journal of Occupational Psychology, 5,* 95-107.

Appelbaum, E., & Batt, R. (1994). *The new American workplace: Transforming work systems in the United States.* Ithaca, NY: ILR.

Argyris, C. (1964). *Integrating the individual and the organization.* New York: John Wiley.

Aronsson, G. (1989). Dimensions of control as related to work organization, stress and health. *International Journal of Health Services, 19,* 459-468.

Asplund, C. (1981). *Redesigning jobs: Western European experience.* Brussels: European Trade Institute.

Atkinson, J. (1985). *Flexibility, uncertainty, and manpower management* (IMS Rep. No. 89). London: Institute of Manpower Studies.

Babbage, C. (1835). *On the economy of machinery and manufacturers.* London: Charles Knight.

Badham, R., Couchman, R. P., & Selden, D. (1996). Winning the socio-technical wager: Change roles and the implementation of self-managing work cells. In R. J. Koubek & W. Karwowski (Eds.), *Manufacturing agility and hybrid automation* (Vol. 1, pp. 339-343). Louisville, KY: IEA.

Baltes, P. B., & Schaie, K. W. (1973). *Lifespan developmental psychology: Personality and socialization.* New York: Academic Press.

Barling, J., & Gallagher, D. G. (1996). Part-time employment. In C. L. Cooper & I. T. Robertson (Eds.), *International review of industrial and organizational psychology* (Vol. 11, pp. 243-278). New York: John Wiley.

Baroudi, J. J., Olson, M. H., & Ives, B. (1986). An empirical study of the impact of user-involvement on system usage and information satisfaction. *Communications of the ACM, 29,* 232-238.

Bates, R. A., & Holton, E. F. (1995). Computerized performance monitoring: A review of human-resource issues. *Human Resource Management Review, 5,* 267-288.

Beaumont, P. B. (1993). *Human resource management: Key concepts and skills.* Newbury Park, CA: Sage.

Becker, H. S., & Geer, B. (1958). The fate of idealism in medical school. *American Sociological Review, 23,* 50-56.

Beehr, T. A. (1976). Perceived situational moderators of the relationship between subjective role ambiguity and role strain. *Journal of Applied Psychology, 61,* 35-40.

Beekun, R. I. (1989). Assessing the effectiveness of sociotechnical interventions: Antidote or fad? *Human Relations, 10,* 877-897.

Beer, M., Eisenstat, R. A., & Spector, B. (1990, November-December). Why change programs don't produce change. *Harvard Business Review, 68,* 158-166.

Belbin, E., & Belbin, R. M. (1972). *Problems in adult retraining.* London: Heinemann.

Belous, R. (1989, March). How human resource systems adjust to the shift towards contingent workers. *Monthly Labor Review,* pp. 7-12.

Bennett, A. (1990). *The death of the organization man.* New York: Simon & Schuster.

Berger, A. (1994). Balancing technological, organizational, and human aspects in manufacturing development. *International Journal of Human Factors in Manufacturing, 4,* 261-280.

Berlinger, L. R., Glick, W. H., & Rodgers, R. C. (1988). Job enrichment and performance improvements. In J. P. Campbell & R. J. Campbell (Eds.), *Productivity in organizations.* San Francisco: Jossey-Bass.

Birchall, D. (1975). *Job design: A planning and implementation guide for managers.* Surrey, UK: Gower.

Birnbaum, P. H., Farh, J., & Wong, G. Y. Y. (1986). The job characteristics model in Hong Kong. *Journal of Applied Psychology, 71,* 598-605.

Blatti, S. (1996). Participative methods to support technical and organizational change for improved competitiveness. In R. J. Koubek & W. Karwowski (Eds.), *Manufacturing agility and hybrid automation* (Vol. 1, pp. 399-402). Louisville, KY: IEA.

Blau, G. J., & Katerberg, R. (1982). Towards enhancing research with the social information processing approach to job design. *Academy of Management Review, 7,* 543-550.

Blauner, R. (1964). *Alienation and freedom: The factory worker and his industry.* Chicago: University of Chicago Press.

Block, L. K., & Stokes, G. S. (1989). Performance and satisfaction in private versus nonprivate work settings. *Environment and Behavior, 21,* 277-297.

Borman, W. C., & Motowidlo, S. J. (1993). Expanding the criteria domain to include elements of contextual performance. In N. Schmitt & W. C. Borman (Eds.), *Personnel selection in organizations* (pp. 71-98). San Francisco: Jossey-Bass.

Bottger, P. C., & Chew, I. K-H. (1986). The job characteristics model and growth satisfaction: Main effects of assimilation of work experience and context satisfaction. *Human Relations, 39,* 575-594.

Brass, D. J. (1979). *Effects of relationships among task positions on job characteristics, interpersonal variables, and employee satisfaction and performance.* Unpublished doctoral dissertation, University of Illinois at Urbana-Champaign.

Bratton, J. (1993). Cellular manufacturing: Some human resource implications. *International Journal of Human Factors in Manufacturing, 3,* 381-399.

Braverman, H. (1974). *Labor and monopoly capital: The degradation of work in the twentieth century.* New York: Monthly Review.

Breaugh, J. A., & Colihan, J. P. (1994). Measuring facets of job ambiguity: Construct-validity evidence. *Journal of Applied Psychology, 79,* 191-202.

Brenner, O. C., Tomkiewicz, J., & Schein, V. E. (1989). The relationship between sex-role stereotypes and requisite management characteristics revisited. *Academy of Management Journal, 32,* 662-669.

Bridges, W. (1994). The end of the job. *Fortune, 130*(6), 62.

British Broadcasting Corporation. (Producer). (1995). *People's century.* London: Producer.

Brockner, J., Konovsky, M., Cooperschneider, R., Folger, R., & Marbies, R. J. (1994). Interactive effects of procedural justice and outcome negativity on victims and survivors of job loss. *Academy of Management Journal, 37,* 397-409.

Brousseau, K. R. (1983). Toward a dynamic model of job-person relationships: Findings, research questions, and implications for work system design. *Academy of Management Review, 8,* 33-45.

Buchanan, D. A. (1979). *The development of job design theories and techniques.* Aldershot: Saxon House.

Buchanan, D. A. (1987, May). High performance: Long live high performance work design! *Personnel Management,* pp. 40-43.

Buchanan, D. A., & Bessant, J. (1985). Failure, uncertainty, and control: The role of operators in a computer integrated production system. *Journal of Management Studies, 22,* 292-308.

Buchanan, D. A., & Boddy, D. (1982). Advanced technology and the quality of working life: The effects of word processing on video typists. *Journal of Occupational Psychology, 55,* 1-11.

Buchanan, D. A., & Boddy, D. (1983). Advanced technology and the quality of working life: The effects of computerized controls on biscuit-making operators. *Journal of Occupational Psychology, 56,* 109-119.

Buchanan, D. A., & McCalman, J. (1989). *High performance work systems: The Digital experience.* New York: Routledge.

Burbidge, J. T. (1979). *Group technology in the engineering industry.* London: Mechanical Engineering Publications.

Burnett, I. (1925). *An experimental investigation into repetitive work* (Industrial Fatigue Research Board, Rep. No. 30). London: HMSO.

Burns, T., & Stalker, G. M. (1961). *The management of innovation.* London: Tavistock.

Cameron, K. S., Mishra, A. K., & Freeman, S. J. (1992). Organizational downsizing. In G. P. Huber & W. H. Glick (Eds.), *Organizational change and redesign.* New York: Oxford University Press.

Campion, M. A. (1988). Interdisciplinary approaches to job design: A constructive replication with extensions. *Journal of Applied Psychology, 73,* 467-481.

Campion, M. A. (1989). Ability requirement implications of job design: An interdisciplinary perspective. *Personnel Psychology, 42,* 1-24.

Campion, M. A., & Berger, C. J. (1990). Conceptual integration and empirical test of job design and compensation relationships. *Personnel Psychology, 43,* 525-553.

Campion, M. A., & McClelland, C. L. (1993). Follow-up and extension of the inter-disciplinary costs and benefits of enlarged jobs. *Journal of Applied Psychology, 78,* 339-351.

Campion, M. A., Medsker, G. J., & Higgs, A. C. (1993). Relations between work group characteristics and effectiveness: Implications for designing effective work groups. *Personnel Psychology, 46,* 823-850.

Campion, M. A., Papper, E. M., & Medsker, G. J. (1996). Relations between work team characteristics and effectiveness: A replication and extension. *Personnel Psychology, 49,* 429-452.

Campion, M. A., & Thayer, P. W. (1985). Development and field evaluation of an interdisciplinary measure of job design. *Journal of Applied Psychology, 70,* 29-43.

Campion, M. A., & Thayer, P. W. (1987). Job design: Approaches, outcomes, and trade-offs. *Organizational Dynamics, 15,* 66-79.

Carayon, P. (1993). A longitudinal test of Karasek's job strain model among office workers. *Work and Stress, 7,* 299-314.

Carey, M. L., & Hazelbaker, K. L. (1986). Employment growth in the temporary help industry. *Monthly Labor Review, 109*(4), 37-44.

Cargille, K. (1995). The up side of downsizing. *Library Acquisitions: Practice and Theory, 19,* 53-57.

Cauldron, S. (1992, November). Working at home pays off. *Personnel Journal,* pp. 40-49.

Chalykoff, J., & Kochan, T. A. (1989). Computer-aided monitoring: Its influence on employee job satisfaction and turnover. *Personnel Psychology, 42,* 807-834.

Champoux, J. E. (1981). The moderating effect of work context satisfaction on the curvilinear relationship between job scope and affective responses. *Human Relations, 34,* 503-515.

Cherns, A. B. (1976). The principles of socio-technical design. *Human Relations, 29,* 783-792.

Cherns, A. B. (1987). The principles of socio-technical design revisited. *Human Relations, 40,* 153-162.

Cherns, A. B., & Davis, L. E. (1975). Assessment of the state of the art. In L. E. Davis & A. B. Cherns (Eds.), *The quality of working life* (Vol. 1). New York: Free Press.

Child, J. (1984). The design of jobs and work structures. In J. Child (Ed.), *Organization: Guide to problems and practice* (2nd ed., pp. 23-55). New York: Harper & Row.

Child, J., & Partridge, B. (1982). *Lost managers.* New York: Cambridge University Press.

Clegg, C. W. (1984). The derivation of job designs. *Journal of Occupational Behavior, 5,* 131-146.

Clegg, C. W. (1988). Appropriate technology for humans and organizations. *Journal of Information Technology, 3,* 133-146.

Clegg, C., Axtell, C. M., Damodaran, L., Farbey, B., Hull, R., Lloyd-Jones, R., Nicholls, J., Sell, R., Tomlinson, C., Ainger, A., & Stewart, T. (1997). Information technology: A study of performance and the role of human and organizational factors. *Ergonomics, 40,* 851-871.

Clegg, C., Carey, N., Dean, G., Hornby, P., & Bolden, R. (1997). Users' reactions to information technology: Some multivariate models and their implications. *Journal of Information Technology, 12,* 15-32.

Clegg, C., Coleman, P., Hornby, P., Maclaren, R., Robson, J., Carey, N., & Symon, G. (1996). Tools to incorporate some psychological and organizational issues during the development of computer-based systems. *Ergonomics, 39,* 482-511.

Clegg, C. W., & Fitter, M. (1978). Information systems: The Achilles heel of job redesign? *Personnel Review, 7,* 5-11.

Clegg, C. W., & Ulich, E. (1987). Job design. In S. Grief, H. Holling, & N. Nicholson (Eds.), *European handbook of work and organisational psychology.* Munich: Urban & Schwarzenberg.

Clegg, C. W., Waterson, P. E., & Axtell, C. M. (1996). Software development: Knowledge-intensive work organizations. *Behaviour and Information Technology, 15,* 237-249.

Clegg, C. W., Waterson, P. E., & Carey, N. (1994). Computer supported collaborative working: Lessons from elsewhere. *Journal of Information Technology, 9,* 85-98.

Cohen, S. G., & Ledford, G. E., Jr. (1994). The effectiveness of self-managing teams: A quasi-experiment. *Human Relations, 47,* 13-43.

Cohen, S. G., Ledford, G. E., Jr., & Spreitzer, G. M. (1996). A predictive model of self-managing work team effectiveness. *Human Relations, 49,* 643-676.

Conger, J., & Kanungo, R. (1988). The empowerment process: Integrating theory and practice. *Academy of Management Review, 13,* 471-482.

Cook, T. D., Campbell, D. T., & Peracchio, L. (1990). Quasi-experimentation. In M. D. Dunnette & L. M. Hough (Eds.), *Handbook of industrial and organizational psychology.* Palo Alto, CA: Consulting Psychologists.

Cooley, M. (1984). Problems of automation. In T. Lupton (Ed.), *Proceedings of the First International Conference on Human Factors in Manufacturing.* Amsterdam: North Holland.

Coovert, M. D. (1980). Locus of control as a predictor of users' attitudes towards computers, *Psychological Reports, 47,* 1167-1173.

Coovert, M. D. (1995). Technological changes in office jobs: What we know and what we can expect. In A. Howard (Ed.), *The changing nature of work* (pp. 175-208). San Francisco: Jossey-Bass.

Cordery, J. L. (1996). Autonomous work groups and quality circles. In M. A. West (Ed.), *Handbook of work group psychology* (pp. 225-246). New York: John Wiley.

Cordery, J. L., Mueller, W. S., & Smith, L. M. (1991). Attitudinal and behavioral effects of autonomous group working: A longitudinal field study. *Academy of Management Journal, 43,* 464-476.

Cordery, J. L., & Sevastos, P. P. (1993). Responses to the original and the revised Job Diagnostic Survey: Is education a factor in responses to negatively worded items? *Journal of Applied Psychology, 78,* 141-143.

Cordery, J. L., Sevastos, P. P., & Parker, S. K. (1992, July). *Job design, skill utilization, and psychological well-being at work: Preliminary test of a model.* Paper presented at the 15th International Congress of Psychology, Brussels.

Cordery, J. L., & Wall, T. D. (1985). Work design and supervisory practices: A model. *Human Relations, 38,* 425-441.

Cordery, J. L., Wright, B. H., & Wall, T. D. (1997, April). *Towards a more comprehensive and integrated approach to work design: Production uncertainty and self-managing work team performance.* Paper presented at the 12th Annual Conference of the Society for Industrial/ Organizational Psychology, St. Louis, MO.

Cotton, J. L. (1993). *Employee involvement: Method for improving performance and work attitudes.* Newbury Park, CA: Sage.

Cox, T. (1978). *Stress.* New York: Macmillan.

Crosby, P. B. (1979). *Quality is free.* New York: McGraw-Hill.

Cross, M. (1986). Multiskilling: Costs and benefits. *Work Study, 35*(4), 23-27.

Crouter, A. C. (1984). Participative work as an influence on human development. *Journal of Applied Developmental Psychology, 5,* 71-90.

Cummings, T. G. (1978). Self-regulating work groups: A socio-technical synthesis. *Academy of Management Review, 3,* 625-634.

Cummings, T. G., & Blumberg, M. (1987). Advanced manufacturing technology and work design. In T. D. Wall, C. W. Clegg, & N. J. Kemp (Eds.), *The human side of advanced manufacturing technology* (pp. 37-60). New York: John Wiley.

Cummings, T. G., Molloy, E. S., & Glen, R. (1977). A methodological critique of fifty-eight selected work experiments. *Human Relations, 30,* 675-708.

Davidson, M. J., & Burke, R. J. (Eds.). (1994). *Women in management: Current research issues.* London: Paul Chapman.

Davies, D. R., & Sparrow, P. R. (1985). Age and work behavior. In N. Charness (Ed.), *Aging and human performance* (pp. 293-332). New York: John Wiley.

Davis, D. D. (1995). Form, function and strategy in boundaryless organizations. In A. Howard (Ed.), *The changing nature of work* (pp. 112-138). San Francisco: Jossey-Bass.

Davis, L. E. (1971). Readying the unready: Post-industrial jobs. *California Management Review, 13,* 27-36.

Davis, L. E., & Canter, R. R. (1956). Job design research. *Journal of Industrial Engineering, 7,* 275-282.

Davis, L. E., Canter, R. R., & Hoffman, J. (1955). Current job design criteria. *Journal of Industrial Engineering, 6,* 5-11.

Davis, L. E., & Taylor, J. C. (1972). *Design of jobs.* Baltimore: Penguin.

Davis, L. E., & Wacker, G. J. (1987). Job design. In G. Salvendy (Ed.), *Handbook of human factors* (pp. 431-445). New York: John Wiley.

Davis-Blake, A., & Uzzi, B. (1993). Employment externalization: The case of temporary workers and independent contractors. *Administrative Science Quarterly, 38,* 195-223.

Dean, J. W., & Snell, S. A. (1991). Integrated manufacturing and job design: Moderating effects of organizational inertia. *Academy of Management Journal, 34,* 774-804.

Delbridge, R., & Turnbull, P. (1992). Human resource maximization: The management of labor under just-in-time manufacturing systems. In P. Blyton & P. Turnbull (Eds.), *Reassessing human resource management.* Newbury Park, CA: Sage.

Delbridge, R., Turnbull, P., & Wilkinson, B. (1992). Pushing back the frontiers: Management control and work intensification under JIT/TQM regimes. *New Technology, Work and Employment, 7,* 97-105.

Dennis, A. R., George, J. F., Jessup, L. M., Nunamaker, J. F., & Vogel, D. R. (1988, December). Information technology to support electronic meetings. *MIS Quarterly,* pp. 591-618.

Dressel, P. L., & Francis, J. (1987). Office productivity: Contributions of the work station. *Behaviour and Information Technology, 6,* 279-284.

Drucker, P. F. (1990). The emerging theory of manufacturing. *Harvard Business Review, 68,* 94-102.

Dunham, R. B., Aldag, R., & Brief, A. (1977). Dimensionality of task design as measured by the Job Diagnostic Survey. *Academy of Management Journal, 20,* 209-223.

Dunphy, D., & Bryant, B. (1996). Teams: Panaceas or prescriptions for improved performance. *Human Relations, 49,* 677-699.

Emery, F. E. (1959). *Characteristics of socio-technical systems* (Document No. 527). London: Tavistock Institute of Human Relations.

Emery, F. E. (1980). Designing socio-technical systems for "greenfield sites." *Journal of Occupational Behavior, 1,* 19-27.

Emery, F. E., & Trist, E. L. (1960). Socio-technical systems. In C. H. Churchman & M. Verhulst (Eds.), *Management science, models and techniques* (Vol. 2, pp. 83-97). New York: Pergamon.

Endler, N. S., & Magnusson, D. (1976). *Interactional psychology and personality.* Washington, DC: Hemisphere.

Ephlin, D. F. (1988, February). Devolution by evolution: The changing relationship between GM and UAW. *Academy of Management Executive, 2*(1), 63-66.

Ettlie, J. E. (1988). *Taking charge of manufacturing.* San Francisco: Jossey-Bass.

Evans, M. G., & Ondrack, D. A. (1991). The motivational potential of jobs: Is a multiplicative model necessary? *Psychological Reports, 69,* 659-672.

Feldman, D. (1990). Reconceptualizing the nature and consequences of part-time work. *Academy of Management Review, 115,* 103-112.

Fletcher, B. C., & Jones, F. (1993). A refutation of Karasek's demand-discretion model of occupational stress with a range of dependent measures. *Journal of Organizational Behavior, 14,* 319-330.

Fox, M. L., Dwyer, D. J., & Ganster, D. C. (1993). Effects of stressful job demands and control on physiological and attitudinal outcomes in a hospital setting. *Academy of Management Journal, 36,* 289-318.

Fraser, R. (1947). *The incidence of neurosis among factory workers* (Industrial Health Research Board, Rep. No. 90). London: HMSO.

Frese, M. (1982). Occupational socialization and psychological development: An underemphasized perspective in industrial psychology. *Journal of Occupational Psychology, 55,* 209-224.

Frese, M. (1989). Theoretical models of control and health. In S. L. Sauter, J. J. Hurrell, Jr., & C. L. Cooper (Eds.), *Job control and worker health* (pp. 108-128). New York: John Wiley.

Frese, M., Fay, D., Hilburger, T., Leng, K., & Tag, A. (1997). The concept of personal initiative: Operationalization, reliability and validity in two German samples. *Journal of Occupational and Organizational Psychology, 70,* 139-161.

Frese, M., Kring, W., Soose, A., & Zempel, J. (1996). Personal initiative at work: Differences between East and West Germany. *Academy of Management Journal, 39,* 37-63.

Frese, M., & Stewart, J. (1984). Skill learning as a concept in life-span developmental psychology: An action theoretic analysis. *Human Development, 27,* 145-162.

Frese, M., Stewart, J., & Hannover, B. (1987). Goal orientation and planfulness: Action styles as personality concepts. *Journal of Personality and Social Psychology, 52,* 1182-1194.

Frese, M., & Zapf, D. (1994). Action as the core of work psychology: A German approach. In H. C. Triandis, M. D. Dunnette, & J. M. Hough (Eds.), *Handbook of industrial and organizational psychology* (Vol. 4, 2nd ed., pp. 271-340). Palo Alto, CA: Consulting Psychologists.

Fried, Y., & Ferris, G. R. (1986). The dimensionality of job characteristics: Some neglected issues. *Journal of Applied Psychology, 71,* 419-426.

Fried, Y., & Ferris, G. R. (1987). The validity of the job characteristics model: A review and meta-analysis. *Personnel Psychology, 40,* 287-322.

Fullerton, H. N., Jr. (1993, November). Another look at the labor force. *Monthly Labor Review,* pp. 31-40.

Ganster, D. C. (1980). Individual differences and task design: A laboratory experiment. *Organizational Behavior and Human Performance, 26,* 131-148.

Garrahan, P., & Stewart, P. (1992). *The Nissan enigma: Flexibility at work in a local community.* London: Mansell.

Geary, J. F. (1992). Pay, control and commitment: Linking appraisal and reward. *Human Resource Management Journal, 2,* 36-54.

George, J. M., & Brief, A. P. (1992). Feeling good—doing good: A conceptual analysis of the mood at work-organizational spontaneity relationship. *Psychological Bulletin, 112,* 310-329.

Gilbert, M. (1996). New technology—old industrial sociology. *New Technology, Work, and Employment, 11,* 3-15.

Gilbreth, F. B. (1911). *Brick laying system.* New York: Clark.

Gladstein, D. (1984). Groups in context: A model of task group effectiveness. *Administrative Science Quarterly, 29,* 499-517.

Goiten, B., & Seashore, S. (1980). *Worker participation: A national survey report.* Ann Arbor: University of Michigan, Survey Research Center.

Goodman, P. S. (1979). *Assessing organizational change: The Rushton quality of work experiment.* New York: John Wiley.

Goodman, P. S., & Dean, J. W., Jr. (1982). Creating long-term organizational change. In P. S. Goodman (Ed.), *Change in organizations: New perspectives on theory, research, and practice.* San Francisco: Jossey-Bass.

Goodman, P. S., Devadas, R., & Griffith-Hughson, T. L. (1988). Groups and productivity: Analyzing the effectiveness of self-managing teams. In J. P. Campbell, R. J. Campbell, & Associates (Eds.), *Productivity in organizations* (pp. 295-327). San Francisco: Jossey-Bass.

Goodman, P. S., Ravlin, E. C., & Schminke, M. (1987). Understanding groups in organizations. In B. M. Staw & L. L. Cummings (Eds.), *Research in organizational behavior* (Vol. 9). Greenwich, CT: JAI.

Graham, I. (1988, Spring). Japanisation as mythology. *Industrial Relations Journal, 19,* 69-75.

Grant, R. A., & Higgins, C. A. (1996). Computerized performance monitors as multidimensional systems: Derivation and application. *ACM Transactions on Information Systems, 14,* 212-235.

Greenberg, E. R. (1988). Downsizing and worker assistance: Latest AMA survey results. *Personnel, 65*(11), 49.

Grey, S. M., & Corlett, E. N. (1989). Creating effective operating teams. In R. Wild (Ed.), *International handbook of production and operations management.* London: Cassell.

Griffin, R. W. (1983). Objective and social sources of information in task design: A field experiment. *Administrative Science Quarterly, 28,* 184-200.

Griffin, R. W. (1991). Effects of work redesign on employee perceptions, attitudes and behaviors: A long-term investigation. *Academy of Management Journal, 34,* 425-435.

Griffin, R. W., Bateman, T. S., Wayne, S. J., & Head, T. C. (1987). Objective and social factors as determinants of task perceptions and responses: An integrated perspective and empirical investigation. *Academy of Management Journal, 30,* 501-523.

Guest, R. H. (1957). Job enlargement: A revolution in job design. *Personnel Administration, 20,* 9-16.

Guzzo, R. A., Jette, R. D., & Katzell, R. A. (1985). The effects of psychologically based intervention programs on worker productivity: A meta-analysis. *Personnel Psychology, 38,* 275-292.

Guzzo, R. A., & Shea, G. P. (1992). Group performance and intergroup relations in organizations. In M. D. Dunnette & L. M. Hough (Eds.), *Handbook of industrial and organizational psychology* (pp. 269-313). Palo Alto, CA: Consulting Psychologists.

Guzzo, R. A., Yost, P. R., Campbell, R. J., & Shea, G. P. (1993). Potency in groups: Articulating a construct. *British Journal of Social Psychology, 32,* 87-106.

Hacker, W. (1986). *Arbeitspsychologie.* Bern: Huber.

Hacker, W., Skell, W., & Straub, W. (1968). *Arbeitspsychologie und wissenschaftlich-technische Revolution.* Berlin: Deutscher Verlag der Wissenschaften.

Hackman, J. R. (1975). On the coming demise of job enrichment. In E. L. Cass & F. G. Zimmer (Eds.), *Man and work in society.* New York: Van Nostrand-Reinhold.

Hackman, J. R. (1977). Work design. In J. R. Hackman & J. L. Suttle (Eds.), *Improving life at work: Behavioral science approaches to organizational change.* Santa Monica, CA: Goodyear.

Hackman, J. R. (1987). The design of work teams. In J. Lorsch (Ed.), *Handbook of organizational behavior* (pp. 315-342). Englewood Cliffs, NJ: Prentice Hall.

Hackman, J. R. (1989). *Groups that work (and those that don't): Creating conditions for effective teamwork.* San Francisco: Jossey-Bass.

Hackman, J. R., & Lawler, E. E. (1971). Employee reactions to job characteristics. *Journal of Applied Psychology, 55,* 259-286.

Hackman, J. R., & Oldham, G. (1975). Development of the Job Diagnostic Survey. *Journal of Applied Psychology, 60,* 159-170.

Hackman, J. R., & Oldham, G. (1976). Motivation through the design of work: Test of a theory. *Organizational Behavior and Human Performance, 16,* 250-279.

Hackman, J. R., & Oldham, G. R. (1980). *Work redesign.* Reading, MA: Addison-Wesley.

Hakamaki, J., & Forssen-Nyberg, M. (1996). Simulation game: A participative method for development. In R. J. Koubek & W. Karwowski (Eds.), *Manufacturing agility and hybrid automation* (Vol. 1, pp. 575-579). Louisville, KY: IEA.

Halton, J. (1985). The anatomy of computing. In T. Forester (Ed.), *The information technology revolution: The complete guide.* Oxford, UK: Basil Blackwell.

Harding, D. W. (1931). A note on the subdivision of assembly work. *Journal of the National Institute of Industrial Psychology, 5,* 261-264.

Harvey, R. J., Billings, R., & Nilan, K. (1985). Confirmatory factor analysis of the Job Diagnostic Survey: Good news and bad news. *Journal of Applied Psychology, 70,* 461-463.

146

JOB AND WORK DESIGN

Hatcher, L., & Ross, T. L. (1991). From individual incentives to an organization-wide gainsharing plan: Effects on teamwork and product quality. *Journal of Organizational Behavior, 12,* 169-183.

Hayes, R., & Jaikumar, R. (1988). Manufacturing's crisis: New technologies, obsolete organizations. *Harvard Business Review, 66,* 77-85.

Hayes, R. H., Wheelwright, S. C., & Clark, K. B. (1988). *Dynamic manufacturing: Creating the learning organization.* New York: Free Press.

Hedberg, B., & Mumford, E. (1975). The design of computer systems. In E. Mumford & H. Sackman (Eds.), *Human choice and computers.* New York: North Holland.

Herbst, P. G. (1974). *Sociotechnical design.* London: Tavistock.

Herzberg, F. (1966). *Work and the nature of man.* Cleveland, OH: World.

Herzberg, F. (1968). One more time: How do you motivate your workers? *Harvard Business Review, 46,* 53-62.

Herzberg, F., Mausner, B., & Snyderman, B. (1959). *The motivation to work.* New York: John Wiley.

Hill, S. (1991). Why quality circles failed but total quality might succeed. *British Journal of Industrial Relations, 29,* 541-568.

Hisrich, R. D. (1990). Entrepreneurship/intrapreneurship. *American Psychologist, 45,* 209-222.

Hochschild, A. (1989). *The second shift.* New York: Viking.

Howard, A. (1995). A framework for work change. In A. Howard (Ed.), *The changing nature of work* (pp. 3-44). San Francisco: Jossey-Bass.

Hughes, D., & Galinsky, E. (1994). Work experiences and marital interactions: Elaborating the complexity of work. *Journal of Organizational Behavior, 13,* 423-438.

Hutchins, E. (1990). The technology of team navigation. In J. Galegher, R. Kraut, & C. Egido (Eds.), *Intellectual teamwork: Social and technological foundations of co-operative work.* Hillsdale, NJ: Lawrence Erlbaum.

Huuhtanen, P., & Leino, T. (1989). Skills and job commitment in high technology industries in the US. *New Technology, Work and Employment, 3,* 112-124.

Huws, U., Podro, S., Gunnarsson, E., Weijers, T., Arvanitaki, K., & Trova, V. (1996). *Teleworking and gender* (Institute of Employment Studies Rep. No. 317). Grantham, UK: Grantham Book Services.

Iaffaldano, M. T., & Muchinsky, P. M. (1985). Job satisfaction and job performance: A meta-analysis. *Psychological Bulletin, 97,* 251-273.

Idaszak, J. R., & Drasgow, F. (1987). A revision of the Job Diagnostic Survey: Elimination of a measurement artefact. *Journal of Applied Psychology, 72,* 69-74.

Idaszak, J. R., Bottom, W. P., & Drasgow, F. (1988). A test of the measurement equivalence of the revised Job Diagnostic Survey: Past problems and current solutions. *Journal of Applied Psychology, 73,* 647-656.

Ilgen, D. R., & Hollenbeck, J. R. (1991). The structure of work: Job design and roles. In M. D. Dunnette & L. M. Hough (Eds.), *Handbook of industrial and organizational psychology* (2nd ed., pp. 165-207). Palo Alto, CA: Consulting Psychologists.

Industrial Health Research Board. (1931). *Annual report.* London: HMSO.

Ingersoll Engineers. (1990). *Competitive manufacturing: The quiet revolution.* Rugby, UK: Author.

Ishikawa, K. (1985). *What is total quality control? The Japanese way.* Englewood Cliffs, NJ: Prentice Hall.

Jackson, P. R., & Martin, R. (1996). Impact of just-in-time on job content, employee attitudes, and well-being: A longitudinal analysis. *Ergonomics, 39,* 1-16.

Jackson, P. R., & Wall, T. D. (1991). How does operator control enhance performance of advanced manufacturing technology? *Ergonomics, 34,* 1301-1311.

Jackson, S. E. (1989). Does job control control job stress? In S. L. Sauter, J. J. Hurrell, Jr., & C. L. Cooper (Eds.), *Job control and worker health.* New York: John Wiley.

Jackson, S., & Schuler, R. (1985). A meta-analysis and conceptual critique of research on role ambiguity and role conflict in work settings. *Organizational Behavior and Human Decision Processes, 36,* 16-78.

Jelinek, M., & Goldhar, J. D. (1984). The strategic implications of the factory of the future. *Sloan Management Review, 25,* 29-37.

Johns, G., Xie, J. L., & Fang, Y. (1992). Mediating and moderating effects in job design. *Journal of Management, 18,* 657-676.

Johnston, W. B., & Packer, A. E. (1987). *Workforce 2000: Work and workers for the twenty-first century.* Indianapolis: Hudson Institute.

Jones, A., & Webb, T. (1987). Introducing computer-integrated manufacturing. *Journal of General Management, 12*(4), 60-74.

Kahn, R., Wolfe, D., Quinn, R., Snoek, J., & Rosenthal, R. (1964). *Occupational stress: Studies in role conflict and ambiguity.* New York: John Wiley.

Kalimo, R., & Vuori, J. (1991). Work factors and health: The predictive role of pre-employment experiences. *Journal of Occupational Psychology, 64,* 97-115.

Kanter, R. M. (1989). *When giants learn to dance.* New York: Simon & Schuster.

Karasek, R. A. (1976). *The impact of the work environment on life outside the job.* Doctoral dissertation, Massachusetts Institute of Technology, distributed by the National Technical Information Service, U.S. Department of Commerce, Springfield, VA 22161 (Thesis Order No. PB 263-073).

Karasek, R. A. (1978, August). *Job socialization: A longitudinal study of work, political activity, and leisure in Sweden.* Paper presented at the Ninth World Congress of Sociology (RC30), Uppsala, Sweden.

Karasek, R. A. (1979). Job demands, job decision latitude and mental strain: Implications for job redesign. *Administrative Science Quarterly, 24,* 285-308.

Karasek, R. A. (1989). The political implications of psychosocial work redesign: A model of the psychosocial class structure. *International Journal of Health Services, 19,* 481-508.

Karasek, R. A. (1990). Lower health risk with increased control among white collar employees. *Journal of Organizational Behavior, 11,* 171-185.

Karasek, R. A., & Theorell, T. (1990). *Healthy work: Stress, productivity, and the reconstruction of working life.* New York: Basic Books.

Karwowski, W., & Associates. (1994). Integrating people, organization, and technology in advanced manufacturing: A position paper based on the joint view of industrial managers, engineers, consultants and researchers. *International Journal of Human Factors in Manufacturing, 4,* 1-19.

Kasl, S. V. (1989). An epidemiological perspective on the role of control on health. In S. L. Sauter, J. J. Hurrell, & C. L. Cooper (Eds.), *Job control and worker health.* New York: John Wiley.

Kelly, J. E. (1978). A reappraisal of socio-technical systems theory. *Human Relations, 31,* 1069-1099.

Kelly, J. E. (1982). *Scientific management, job redesign and work performance.* London: Academic Press.

Kelly, J. E. (1992). Does job re-design theory explain job re-design outcomes? *Human Relations, 45,* 753-774.

Kemp, N. J., Clegg, C. W., & Wall, T. D. (1980). Content, process, and outcomes. *Employee Relations, 2*(5), 5-14.

Kemp, N. J., & Cook, J. D. (1983). Job longevity and growth need strength as joint moderators of the task design-job satisfaction relationship. *Human Relations, 36,* 883-898.

Kemp, N. J., Wall, T. D., Clegg, C. W., & Cordery, J. L. (1983). Autonomous work groups in a greenfield site: A comparative study. *Journal of Occupational Psychology, 56,* 271-288.

Kerr, S., Hill, K. D., & Broedling, L. (1986). The first-line supervisor: Phasing out or here to stay? *Academy of Management Review, 11,* 103-117.

Kessler, I. (1995). Reward systems. In J. Storey (Ed.), *Human resource management: A critical text* (pp. 254-279). New York: Routledge.

Kidd, P. T. (1994). *Agile manufacturing: Forging new frontiers.* Reading, MA: Addison-Wesley.

Kidd, P. T., & Karwowski, W. (1994). *Advances in agile manufacturing: Integrating technology, organization, and people.* Amsterdam: IOS.

Kiesler, S., & Sproull, L. (1992). Group decision making and communication technology. *Organizational Behavior and Human Decision Processes, 52,* 96-123.

King, N. A. (1970). A clarification and evaluation of the two-factor theory of job satisfaction. *Psychological Bulletin, 74,* 18-30.

Kirkman, B. L., Shapiro, D, L., Novelli, L., Jr., & Brett, J. M. (1996). Employee concerns regarding self-managing work teams: A multidimensional perspective. *Social Justice Research, 9*(1), 47-67.

Klein, J. A. (1989, March-April). The human cost of manufacturing reform. *Harvard Business Review, 44,* 61.

Klein, J. A. (1991). A re-examination of autonomy in light of new manufacturing practices. *Human Relations, 44,* 21-38.

Klein, L. (1994). A sociotechnical/organizational design. In W. Karwowski & G. Salvendy (Eds.), *Organization and management of advanced manufacturing.* New York: John Wiley.

Kohn, M. L., & Schooler, C. (1978). The reciprocal effects of the substantive complexity of work on intellectual complexity: A longitudinal assessment. *American Journal of Sociology, 48,* 24-52.

Kohn, M. L., & Schooler, C. (1982). Job conditions and personality: A longitudinal assessment of their reciprocal effects. *American Journal of Sociology, 87,* 1257-1286.

Kompier, M. A. J. (1996). Job design and well-being. In M. J. Schabracq, J. A. M. Winnubst, & C. L. Cooper (Eds.), *Handbook of work and health psychology* (pp. 349-368). New York: John Wiley.

Kopelman, R. E. (1985). Job redesign and productivity: A review of the evidence. *National Productivity Review, 4,* 237-255.

Kornhauser, A. (1965). *Mental health of the industrial worker.* New York: John Wiley.

Kozlowski, S. W. J., Chao, G. T., Smith, E. M., & Hedlund, J. (1993). Organizational downsizing: Strategies, interventions, and research implications. In C. L. Cooper & I. T. Robertson (Eds.), *International review of industrial and organizational psychology* (Vol. 8). New York: John Wiley.

Krausz, M., Brandwein, T., & Fox, S. (1995). Work attitudes and emotional responses of permanent, voluntary, and involuntary temporary-help employees: An exploratory study. *Applied Psychology: An International Review, 44,* 217-232.

Lafitte, F. (1962). Social policy in a free society. In W. D. Birrell, P. A. R. Hillyard, A. S. Murie, & D. J. D. Roche (Eds.), *Social administration.* New York: Penguin.

Landsbergis, P. A. (1988). Occupational stress among health care workers: A test of the job demands-control model. *Journal of Organizational Behavior, 9,* 217-240.

Latham, G. P., Winters, D. C., & Locke, E. A. (1994). Cognitive and motivational effects of participation: A mediator study. *Journal of Organizational Behavior, 15,* 49-63.

Lawler, E. E. (1981). *Pay and organization development.* Reading, MA: Addison-Wesley.

Lawler, E. E. (1986). *High involvement management: Participative strategies for improving organizational performance.* San Francisco: Jossey-Bass.

Lawler, E. E. (1990). *Strategic pay: Aligning organizational strategies and pay systems.* San Francisco: Jossey-Bass.

Lawler, E. E. (1992). *The ultimate advantage: Creating the high involvement organization.* San Francisco: Jossey-Bass.

Lawler, E. E. (1994). From job-based to competency-based organizations. *Journal of Organizational Behavior, 15,* 3-15.

Lawler, E. E., Mohrman, S. A., & Ledford, G. E. (1992). *Employee involvement and total quality management*. San Francisco: Jossey-Bass.

Lawrence, P., & Lorsch, J. (1969). *Organization and environment*. Homewood, IL: Irwin.

Lee, R., & Klein, A. R. (1982). Structure of the Job Diagnostic Survey for public sector organizations. *Journal of Applied Psychology, 67,* 515-519.

Lee, T. W., & Johnson, D. R. (1991). The effects of work schedule and employment status on the organizational commitment and job satisfaction of full-time versus part-time employees. *Journal of Vocational Behavior, 38,* 208-224.

Legge, K. (1995). *Human resource management: Rhetoric and realities*. New York: Macmillan.

Lei, D., & Goldhar, J. D. (1993). The implementation of CIM technology: The key role of organizational learning. *International Journal of Human Factors in Manufacturing, 3,* 217-230.

Lewis, S., & Cooper, C. L. (1987). Stress in dual earner couples and stage in life cycle. *Journal of Occupational Psychology, 60,* 289-303.

Liebowitz, S. J., & DeMeuse, K. P. (1982). The application of team building. *Human Relations, 35,* 1-18.

Liff, S. (1990). Clerical workers and information technology: Gender relations and occupational change. *New Technology, Work and Employment, 5,* 44-55.

Lim, K. Y., Long, J. B., & Silcock, N. (1992). Integrating human factors with the Jackson system development method: An illustrated overview. *Ergonomics, 35,* 1135-1161.

Littler, C. (1985). Taylorism, Fordism, and job design. In D. Knights, H. Wilmott, & D. Collinson (Eds.), *Job redesign: Critical perspectives on the labour process*. Aldershot, UK: Gower.

Littler, C. R., & Salaman, G. (1985). The design of work. In C. R. Littler (Ed.), *The experience of work*. Hampshire, UK: Gower.

Locke, E. A., & Henne, D. (1986). Work motivation theories. In C. L. Cooper & I. T. Robertson (Eds.), *International review of industrial and organizational psychology* (Vol. 2, pp. 1-25). New York: John Wiley.

Locke, E. A., & Schweiger, D. M. (1979). Participation in decision-making: One more look. In B. Staw (Ed.), *Research in organizational behavior* (Vol. 1). Greenwich, CT: JAI.

Loher, B. T., Noe, R. A., Moeller, N. L., & Fitzgerald, M. P. (1985). A meta-analysis of the relation of job characteristics to job satisfaction. *Journal of Applied Psychology, 70,* 280-289.

Majchrzak, A. (1988). *The human side of factory automation*. San Francisco: Jossey-Bass.

Manz, C. C. (1992). Self-leading work teams: Moving beyond self-management myths. *Human Relations, 45,* 1119-1140.

Manz, C. C., & Sims, H. P., Jr. (1993). *Business without bosses: How self-managing teams are building high performance companies*. New York: John Wiley.

Martin, J., & Roberts, C. (1984). *Women and employment: A lifetime perspective*. London: Office of Population Census and Surveys, HMSO.

Martin, R., & Wall, T. D. (1989). Attentional demand and cost responsibility as stressors in shopfloor jobs. *Academy of Management Journal, 32,* 69-86.

Mathieu, J. E., & Zajac, D. M. (1990). A review and meta-analysis of the antecedents, correlates, and consequences of organizational commitment. *Psychological Bulletin, 108,* 171-194.

McCune, J. T., Beatty, R. W., & Montagno, R. V. (1988). Downsizing: Practices in manufacturing firms. *Human Resources Management Journal, 27,* 145-161.

Melamed, S., Ben-Avi, I., Luz, J., & Green, M. S. (1995). Objective and subjective work monotony: Effects on job satisfaction, psychological distress, and absenteeism in blue-collar workers. *Journal of Applied Psychology, 80,* 29-42.

Melcher, R. (1967, May-June). Roles and relationships: Clarifying the manager's job. *Personnel.*

Melvin, J. (1992, November). Office for the 1990s. *Facilities, 10,* 16-19.

Mohrman, S. A., & Cohen, S. G. (1995). When people get out of the box: New relationships, new systems. In A. Howard (Ed.), *The changing nature of work* (pp. 365-410). San Francisco: Jossey-Bass.

Mohrman, S. A., Cohen, S. G., & Mohrman, A. M., Jr. (1995). *Designing team-based organizations: New forms for knowledge and work.* San Francisco: Jossey-Bass.

Mohrman, S., & Mohrman, J. R. (1997). *Designing and leading team-based organizations: A workbook for organizational self-design.* San Francisco: Jossey-Bass.

Montagno, R. V. (1985). The effects of comparison others and prior experience on responses to task design. *Academy of Management Journal, 28,* 491-498.

Motowidlo, S. J., & Van Scotter, J. R. (1994). Evidence that task performance should be distinguished from contextual performance. *Journal of Applied Psychology, 79,* 475-480.

Mottaz, C. (1986). Gender differences in work satisfaction, work-related rewards and values, and the determinants of work satisfaction. *Human Relations, 39,* 359-376.

Mullarkey, S., Jackson, P. R., & Parker, S. K. (1995). Employee reactions to JIT manufacturing practices: A two-phase investigation. *International Journal of Operations and Production Management, 15,* 62-79.

Mumford, E. (1986). *Using computers for business success: The ETHICS method.* Manchester, UK: Manchester Business School.

Nadler, G. (1963). *Work design.* Homewood, IL: Irwin.

Neuman, G. A. (1991). Autonomous work group selection. *Journal of Business and Psychology, 6,* 283-291.

Neumann, J. E., Holti, R., & Standing, H. (1995). *Change everything at once: The Tavistock Institute's guide to developing teamwork in manufacturing.* Oxfordshire, UK: Management Books 2000.

Nicholson, N., & West, M. A. (1988). *Managerial job change: Men and women in transition.* New York: Cambridge University Press.

Oakland, J. S. (1989). *Total quality management.* Oxford, UK: Heinemann.

Organizational Aspects Special Interest Group. (1996). *Failing to deliver: The IT performance gap.* Swindon, UK: Economic and Social Research Council.

Oldham, G. (1976). Job characteristics and internal motivation: The moderating effect of interpersonal and individual variables. *Human Relations, 29,* 559-569.

Oldham, G. R. (1996). Job design. In C. L. Cooper & I. T. Robertson (Eds.), *International review of industrial and organizational psychology* (Vol. 11, pp. 33-60). New York: John Wiley.

Oldham, G. R., & Hackman, J. R. (1980). Work design in the organizational context. In B. Staw & L. L. Cummings (Eds.), *Research in organizational behavior* (Vol. 2). Greenwich, CT: JAI.

Oldham, G. P., Kulik, C. T., Ambrose, M. L., Stepina, L. P., & Brand, J. F. (1986). Relations between job facet comparisons and employee reactions. *Organizational Behavior and Human Decision Processes, 38,* 28-47.

Oldham, G. P., Kulik, C. T., & Stepina, L. P. (1991). Physical environments and employee reactions: Effects of stimulus-screening skills and job complexity. *Academy of Management Journal, 34,* 929-938.

Oldham, G. P., Nottenburg, G., Kassner, M. K., Ferris, G., Fedor, D., & Masters, M. (1982). The selection and consequences of job comparisons. *Organizational Behavior and Human Performance, 29,* 84-111.

Oliver, N. (1991). The dynamics of just-in-time. *New Technology, Work and Employment, 6,* 19-27.

O'Reilly, C. A., & Caldwell, D. F. (1979). Informational influence as a determinant of perceived task characteristics and job satisfaction. *Journal of Applied Psychology, 64,* 157-165.

O'Reilly, C. A., & Caldwell, D. F. (1985). The impact of normative social influence and cohesiveness on task perceptions and attitudes: A social information processing approach. *Journal of Occupational Psychology, 59,* 193-206.

Osterman, P. (1994). How common is workplace transformation and who adopts it? *Industrial and Labor Relations Review, 47,* 173-188.

Ouchi, W. G. (1977). The relationship between organizational structure and organizational control. *Administrative Science Quarterly, 22,* 95-113.

Parker, M., & Slaughter, J. (1988). *Choosing sides: Unions and the team concept.* Boston: South End.

Parker, S. K. (1996). An investigation of attitudes amongst production employees. *International Journal of Human Factors in Manufacturing, 6,* 281-303.

Parker, S. K. (in press). Enhancing role breadth self-efficacy: The role of job enrichment and other organizational interventions. *Journal of Applied Psychology.*

Parker, S. K., Chmiel, N., & Wall, T. D. (1997). Work characteristics and employee well-being within a context of strategic downsizing. *Journal of Occupational Health Psychology, 2,* 289-303.

Parker, S. K., & Jackson, P. R. (1993). The implementation of high performance work teams. In D. Gowler, K. Legge, & C. Clegg (Eds.), *Case studies in organisational behaviour and human resource management* (2nd ed., pp. 42-56). London: Paul Chapman.

Parker, S. K., & Jackson, P. R. (1994). Facilitating new shopfloor roles within modern manufacturing. In P. T. Kidd & W. Karwowski (Eds.), *Advances in agile manufacturing: Integrating technology, organization, and people* (pp. 157-160). Amsterdam: IOS.

Parker, S. K., Jackson, P. R., Sprigg, C. A., & Whybrow, A. (1996). New production initiatives: Minimizing risk and maximizing potential. In R. J. Koubek & W. Karwowski (Eds.), *Manufacturing agility and hybrid automation* (Vol. 1, pp. 127-130). Louisville, KY: IEA.

Parker, S. K., Mullarkey, S., & Jackson, P. R. (1994). Dimensions of performance effectiveness in high-involvement work organizations. *Human Resource Management Journal, 4,* 1-21.

Parker, S. K., Myers, C., & Wall, T. D. (1995). The effects of a manufacturing initiative on employee jobs and strain. In S. A. Robertson (Ed.), *Contemporary ergonomics 1995* (pp. 37-42). New York: Taylor & Francis.

Parker, S. K., Sprigg, C. A., & Wall, T. D. (1998). *Being a temporary employee: Something to smile about?* Unpublished manuscript.

Parker, S. K., & Wall, T. D. (1996). Job design and modern manufacturing. In P. B. Warr (Ed.), *Psychology at work* (4th ed., pp. 333-358). New York: Penguin.

Parker, S. K., Wall, T. D., & Jackson, P. R. (1994). Job design and work orientations in modern manufacturing: A comparative case study. In S. A. Robertson (Ed.), *Contemporary ergonomics 1994* (pp. 411-416). New York: Taylor & Francis.

Parker, S. K., Wall, T. D., & Jackson, P. R. (1997). "That's not my job": Developing flexible employee work orientations. *Academy of Management Journal, 40,* 899-929.

Parnaby, J. (1988). A systems approach to the implementation of JIT methodologies in Lucas Industries. *International Journal of Production Research, 26,* 483-492.

Pasmore, W. A. (1978). The comparative impacts of sociotechnical system, job redesign and survey-feedback interventions. In W. A. Pasmore & J. Sherwood (Eds.), *Sociotechnical systems: A source book.* San Diego: University Associates.

Pasmore, W. A. (1988). *Designing effective organizations: The sociotechnical systems perspective.* New York: John Wiley.

Pasmore, W., Francis, C., Haldeman, J., & Shani, A. (1982). Socio-technical systems: A North American reflection on the empirical studies of the seventies. *Human Relations, 35,* 1179-1204.

Paul, W. P., & Robertson, K. B. (1970). *Job enrichment and employee motivation.* London: Gower.

Pauling, T. P. (1968). Job enlargement: An experience at Phillips Telecommunications of Australia Limited. *Personnel Practice Bulletin, 24,* 194-196.

Pearce, J. A., & Ravlin, E. C. (1987). The design and activation of self-regulating work groups. *Human Relations, 40,* 751-782.

Perrow, C. (1967). A framework for the comparative analysis of organizations. *American Sociological Review, 32,* 194-208.

Phillimore, A. J. (1989). Flexible specialisation, work organisation and skills: Approaching the "second industrial divide." *New Technology, Work and Employment, 4,* 79-91.

Pine, B. J. (1993). Customizing for the new consumer. *Fortune, 128,* 45.

Piore, M., & Sabel, C. (1984). *The second industrial divide: Possibilities for prosperity.* New York: Basic Books.

Podsakoff, P. M., & Williams, J. J. (1986). The relationship between job performance and job satisfaction. In E. A. Locke (Ed.), *Generalizing from laboratory to field settings.* Lexington, MA: Lexington.

Pontusson, J. (1990). The politics of new technology and job redesign: A comparison of Volvo and British-Leyland. *Economic and Industrial Democracy, 11,* 311-336.

Rice, A. K. (1958). *Productivity and social organization.* London: Tavistock.

Rice, R. W., Frone, M. R., & McFarlin, D. B. (1992). Work non-work conflict and the perceived quality of life. *Journal of Organizational Behavior, 13,* 155-168.

Roberts, K. H., & Glick, W. (1981). The job characteristics approach to job design: A critical review. *Journal of Applied Psychology, 66,* 193-217.

Rose, M. (1975). *Industrial behavior.* New York: Penguin.

Rosen, B., & Jerdee, T. H. (1977). Too old or not too old? *Harvard Business Review, 7*(6), 97-108.

Rotchford, N. L., & Roberts, K. H. (1982). Part-time workers as missing persons in organizational research. *Academy of Management Review, 2,* 228-234.

Rousseau, D. M., & Wade-Benzoni, K. A. (1995). Changing individual-organization attachments: A two-way street. In A. Howard (Ed.), *The changing nature of work* (pp. 290-322). San Francisco: Jossey-Bass.

Roxburgh, S. (1996). Gender differences in work and well-being: Effects of exposure and vulnerability. *Journal of Health and Social Behavior, 37,* 265-277.

Russell, B. (1995). The subtle labor process and the great skill debate: Evidence from a potash mine-mill operation. *Canadian Journal of Sociology, 20,* 359-385.

Russell-Gardner, C., & Jackson, P. (1995). Workforce flexibility: Workforce reactions. In Division and Section of Occupational Psychology (Ed.), *Proceedings of the Annual British Psychological Society Occupational Psychology Conference* (pp. 297-302). Leicester, UK: British Psychological Society.

Safizadeh, M. H. (1991, Summer). The case of work groups in manufacturing operations. *California Management Review,* pp. 61-82.

Salancik, G. R., & Pfeffer, J. (1978). A social information processing approach to job attitudes and task design. *Administrative Science Quarterly, 23,* 224-253.

Sawyer, J. E. (1992). Goal and process clarity: Specification of multiple constructs of role ambiguity and a structural equation model of their antecedents and consequences. *Journal of Applied Psychology, 77,* 130-142.

Schein, E. H. (1969). *Process consultation: Its role in organizational development.* Reading, MA: Addison-Wesley.

Schein, V. E. (1994). Managerial sex typing: A persistent and pervasive barrier to women's opportunities. In M. J. Davidson & R. J. Burke (Eds.), *Women in management: Current research issues* (pp. 41-52). London: Paul Chapman.

Scherer, E., & Weik, S. (1996). Autonomy and control in decentralized production systems. In R. J. Koubek & W. Karwowski (Eds.), *Manufacturing agility and hybrid automation* (Vol. 1, pp. 403-406). Louisville, KY: IEA.

Schleicher, R. (1973). Intelligenzleistungen Erwachsener in Abhangigkeit vom Niveau vberuflicher Tatigkeit. *Probleme und Ergebnisse der Psychologie, 44,* 24-25.

Schnake, M. E., & Dumler, M. P. (1985). Affective response bias in the measurement of perceived task characteristics. *Journal of Occupational Psychology, 58,* 159-166.

Schonberger, R. J. (1986). *World class manufacturing: The lessons of simplicity applied.* New York: Free Press.

Schwartz, F. N. (1988). Corporate women: A critical business resource. *Vital Speeches, 54,* 173-176.

Scully, J. A., Kirkpatrick, S. A., & Locke, E. A. (1995). Locus of knowledge as a determination of the effects of participation on performance, affect, and perceptions. *Organizational Behavior and Human Decision Processes, 61,* 276-288.

Seeborg, I. (1978). The influence of employee participation in job redesign. *Journal of Applied Behavioral Science, 14,* 87-98.

Senge, P. M. (1990). *The fifth discipline: The age and practice of the learning organization.* London: Century Business.

Sewell, G., & Wilkinson, B. (1992). Empowerment or emasculation? Shopfloor surveillance in a total quality organization. In P. Blyton & P. Turnbull (Eds.), *Reassessing human resource management.* Newbury Park, CA: Sage.

Shaiken, H. (1979). *Impact of new technology on employees and their organizations: Research report.* Berlin: International Institute for Comparative Social Research.

Sharit, J., Chang, T. C., & Salvendy, G. (1987). Technical and human aspects of computer-aided manufacturing. In G. Salvendy (Ed.), *Handbook of human factors.* New York: John Wiley.

Shea, G. P., & Guzzo, R. A. (1987). Groups as human resources. *Research in Personnel and Human Resources Management, 5,* 323-356.

Sonnentag, S. (1996). Work group factors and individual well-being. In M. A. West (Ed.), *Handbook of work group psychology* (pp. 345-370). New York: John Wiley.

Spector, P. E. (1985). Higher-order need strength as a moderator of the job scope-employee outcome relationship: A meta-analysis. *Journal of Occupational Psychology, 58,* 119-127.

Spector, P. E. (1992). A consideration of the validity and meaning of self-report measures of job conditions. In C. L. Cooper & I. T. Robertson (Eds.), *International review of industrial and organizational psychology* (Vol. 7). New York: John Wiley.

Spector, P. E., Brannick, M. T., & Coovert, M. D. (1989). Job analysis. In C. L. Cooper & I. T. Robertson (Eds.), *International review of industrial and organizational psychology* (Vol. 4). New York: John Wiley.

Spector, P. E., & O'Connell, B. J. (1994). The contribution of personality traits, negative affectivity, locus of control and Type A as to the subsequent reports of job stressors and job strains. *Journal of Occupational and Organizational Psychology, 67,* 1-11.

Spreitzer, G. M. (1995). Psychological empowerment in the workplace: Dimensions, measurement, and validation. *Academy of Management Journal, 38,* 1442-1465.

Sprigg, C. A., Jackson, P. R., & Parker, S. K. (1997, April). *The differential impact of teamworking in the same company.* Paper presented at the International Workshop on Teamworking, Nottingham, UK.

Sprigg, C. A., Parker, S. K., & Jackson, P. R. (1996, June). *Effective implementation of team working on the shopfloor.* Paper presented at the Second International Conference on Managing Integrated Manufacturing: Strategic, Organisation and Social Change, Leicester, UK.

Srivastva, S., Salipante, P., Cummings, T., Notz, W., Bigelow, J., & Waters, J. (1975). *Job satisfaction and productivity.* Kent, OH: Kent State University Press.

Sterns, H. L. (1986). Training and retraining adult and older adult workers. In J. E. Birren, P. K. Robinson, & J. E. Livingston (Eds.), *Age, health and employment.* Englewood Cliffs, NJ: Prentice Hall.

Sterns, H. L., & Doverspike, D. (1989). Aging and the training and learning process. In I. L. Goldstein (Ed.), *Training and development in organizations.* San Francisco: Jossey-Bass.

Stevens, M. J., & Campion, M. A. (1994). The knowledge, skills, and ability requirements for teamwork: Implications for human resource management. *Journal of Management, 20,* 503-530.

Stone, E. F. (1986). Job scope-job satisfaction and job scope-job performance relationships. In E. A. Locke (Ed.), *Generalizing from laboratory to field settings.* Lexington, MA: Lexington.

Stone, E. F., & Gueutal, H. G. (1985). An empirical derivation of the dimensions along which characteristics of jobs are perceived. *Academy of Management Journal, 28,* 376-396.

Stone, E. F., Mowday, R. T., & Porter, L. W. (1977). Higher-order need strengths as moderators of the job scope-job satisfaction relationship. *Journal of Applied Psychology, 62,* 466-471.

Storey, J. (1994). *New wave manufacturing strategies: Organizational and human resource management dimensions.* London: Paul Chapman.

Susman, G., & Chase, R. (1986). A sociotechnical systems analysis of the integrated factory. *Journal of Applied Behavioral Science, 22,* 257-270.

Taber, T. D., Beehr, T. A., & Walsh, J. T. (1985). Relationship between job evaluation ratings and self-ratings of job characteristics. *Organizational Behavior and Human Decision Processes, 35,* 27-45.

Taber, T. D., & Taylor, E. (1990). A review and evaluation of the psychometric properties of the Job Diagnostic Survey. *Personnel Psychology, 43,* 467-500.

Tailby, S., & Turnbull, P. (1987, January). Learning to manage just-in-time. *Personnel Management,* pp. 16-19.

Tannenbaum, S. I., Salas, E., & Cannon-Bowers, J. A. (1996). Promoting team effectiveness. In M. A. West (Ed.), *Handbook of work group psychology* (pp. 503-530). New York: John Wiley.

Taylor, F. W. (1911). *The principles of scientific management.* New York: Harper.

Taylor, J. C. (1977). Experiments in work system design: Economic and human results (Parts 1 & 2). *Personnel Review, 6,* 21-42.

Taylor, J. C. (1979). Job design criteria twenty years later. In L. E. Davis & J. C. Taylor (Eds.), *Design of jobs* (2nd ed.). Santa Monica, CA: Goodyear.

Tesluk, P. (1997, April). *Work team technology management: Implications for team effectiveness.* Paper presented at the 12th Annual Conference of the Society for Industrial/Organizational Psychology, St. Louis, MO.

Tetzeli, R. (1994, July 11). Surviving information overload. *Fortune,* pp. 60-65.

Thomas, J., & Griffin, R. W. (1983). The social information processing model of task design: A review of the literature. *Academy of Management Review, 8,* 672-692.

Thomas, K. W., & Velthouse, B. A. (1990). Cognitive elements of empowerment: An "interpretive" model of intrinsic task motivation. *Academy of Management Review, 15,* 666-681.

Thomas, L. T., & Ganster, D. C. (1995). Impact of family-supportive work variables on work-family conflict and strain: A control perspective. *Journal of Applied Psychology, 80,* 6-15.

Thompson, J. (1967). *Organizations in action.* New York: McGraw-Hill.

Thornley, D. H., & Valentine, G. A. (1968). Job enlargement: Some implications of longer cycle jobs on fan heater production. *Phillips Personnel Management Review,* pp. 12-17.

Tolliday, S., & Zeitlin, J. (1986). Introduction: Between Fordism and flexibility. In S. Tolliday & J. Zeitlin (Eds.), *Between Fordism and flexibility.* Oxford, UK: Basil Blackwell.

Tombaugh, J. R., & White, L. P. (1990). Downsizing: An empirical assessment of survivors' perceptions in a post-layoff environment. *Organizational Development Journal, 8,* 32-43.

Trist, E. L., & Bamforth, K. W. (1951). Some social and psychological consequences of the long-wall method of coal-getting. *Human Relations, 4,* 3-38.

Trist, E. L., Susman, G., & Brown, G. W. (1977). An experiment in autonomous group working in an American underground coal mine. *Human Relations, 30,* 201-236.

Turnbull, P. J. (1988). The limits to "Japanisation": Just-in-time, labour relations and the UK automotive industry. *New Technology, Work and Employment, 3,* 7-20.

Turner, A. N., & Lawrence, P. R. (1965). *Industrial jobs and the worker.* Cambridge, MA: Harvard University Press.

Ulich, E. (1991). *Arbeitpsychologie.* Stuttgart: Poeschel.

U.S. Department of Labor. (1992). *Tabulations from the current population survey.* Washington, DC: Government Printing Office.

Van Beck, H. G. (1964). The influence of assembly line organisation on output, quality and morale. *Occupational Psychology, 38,* 161-72.

Van Cott, H. P. (1985). High technology and human needs. *Ergonomics, 28,* 1135-1142.

Van de Ven, A. H., & Morgan, M. A. (1980). A revised framework for organizational assessment. In E. E. Lawler, D. A. Nadler, & C. Camman (Eds.), *Organizational assessment: Perspectives on the measurement of organizational behavior and the quality of working life.* New York: John Wiley.

Van der Spiegel, J. (1995). New information technologies and changes in work. In A. Howard (Ed.), *The changing nature of work* (pp. 97-111). San Francisco: Jossey-Bass.

Van Maanen, J. (1976). Breaking in: Socialization to work. In R. Dublin (Ed.), *Handbook of work, organization and society* (pp. 67-130). Chicago: Rand McNally.

Venkatesh, A., & Vitalari, N. P. (1992). An emerging distributed work arrangement: An investigation of computer-based supplemental work at home. *Management Science, 38,* 1687-1706.

Vernon, H. M., Wyatt, S., & Ogden, A. D. (1924). *On the extent and effects of variety in repetitive work: Medical Research Council, Industrial Fatigue Research Board report.* London: HMSO.

Volpert, W. (1975). Die Lohnarbeitswissenschaft und die Psychologie der Arbeitstätigkeit. In P. Brobkurth & W. Volpert (Eds.), *Lohnarbeitspsychologie.* Frankfurt am Main: Fischer.

Voss, C. A., & Robinson, S. J. (1987). Application of just-in-time manufacturing techniques in the United Kingdom. *International Journal of Operations and Production Management, 7,* 46-52.

Walker, C. R. (1950). The problem of the repetitive job. *Harvard Business Review, 28,* 54-58.

Walker, C. R., & Guest, R. (1952). *Man on the assembly line.* Cambridge, MA: Harvard University Press.

Wall, T. D. (1996). Working with robots. *Psychologist, 9,* 163-166.

Wall, T. D., & Clegg, C. W. (1981). A longitudinal study of group work redesign. *Journal of Occupational Behavior, 2,* 31-49.

Wall, T. D., Clegg, C. W., & Jackson, P. R. (1978). An evaluation of the job characteristics model. *Journal of Occupational Psychology, 51,* 183-196.

Wall, T. D., Corbett, M. J., Clegg, C. W., Jackson, P. R., & Martin, R. (1990). Advanced manufacturing technology and work design: Towards a theoretical framework. *Journal of Organizational Behavior, 11,* 201-219.

Wall, T. D., Corbett, M. J., Martin, R., Clegg, C. W., & Jackson, P. R. (1990). Advanced manufacturing technology, work design and performance: A change study. *Journal of Applied Psychology, 75,* 691-697.

Wall, T. D., & Davids, K. (1992). Shopfloor work organization and advanced manufacturing technology. In C. L. Cooper & I. Robertson (Eds.), *International review of industrial and organizational psychology* (Vol. 7, pp. 363-398). New York: John Wiley.

Wall, T. D., & Jackson, P. R. (1995). New manufacturing initiatives and shopfloor work design. In A. Howard (Ed.), *The changing nature of work* (pp. 139-174). San Francisco: Jossey-Bass.

Wall, T. D., Jackson, P. R., & Davids, K. (1992). Operator work design and robotics system performance: A serendipitous field study. *Journal of Applied Psychology, 77,* 353-362.

Wall, T. D., Jackson, P. R., Mullarkey, S., & Parker, S. K. (1996). The demands-control model of job strain: A more specific test. *Journal of Occupational and Organizational Psychology, 69,* 153-166.

Wall, T. D., Kemp, N. J., Jackson, P. R., & Clegg, C. W. (1986). An outcome evaluation of autonomous work groups: A long-term field experiment. *Academy of Management Journal, 29,* 280-304.

Wall, T. D., & Martin, R. (1987). Job and work design. In C. L. Cooper & I. T. Robertson (Eds.), *International review of industrial and organizational psychology* (Vol. 3, pp. 61-91). New York: John Wiley.

Wall, T. D., & Stephenson, G. M. (1970). Herzberg's two-factor theory of job attitudes: A critical evaluation and some fresh evidence. *Industrial Relations Journal, 1,* 41-65.

Walton, R. E. (1972, November-December). How to counter alienation in the plant. *Harvard Business Review,* 70-81.

Walton, R. E. (1977). Work innovations at Topeka: After six years. *Journal of Applied Behavioral Science, 13,* 422-433.

Walton, R. (1979, July-August). Work innovations in the United States. *Harvard Business Review,* 88-98.

Walton, R. E. (1982). New perspectives on the world of work. *Human Relations, 35,* 1073-1084.

Walton, R. E. (1985, March-April). From control to commitment in the workplace. *Harvard Business Review,* 77-84.

Walton, R. E., & Susman, G. E. (1987, March-April). People policies for the new machines. *Harvard Business Review,* 98-106.

Warr, P. B. (1990). The measurement of well-being and other aspects of mental health. *Journal of Occupational Psychology, 52,* 129-148.

Warr, P. B. (1994). A conceptual framework for the study of work and mental health. *Work and Stress, 8,* 84-97.

Warr, P. B. (in press). Well-being and the work-place. In D. Kahneman, E. Diener, & N. Schwarz (Eds.), *Understanding quality of life: Scientific perspectives on enjoyment and suffering.* New York: Russell Sage.

Waterson, P. E., Clegg, C. W., Bolden, R., Pepper, K., Warr, P. B., & Wall, T. D. (1997). *The use and effectiveness of modern manufacturing practices in the UK.* Sheffield, UK: Institute of Work Psychology.

Wellins, R. S., Byham, W. C., & Wilson, J. M. (1991). *Empowered teams: Creating self-directed work groups that improve quality, productivity, and participation.* San Francisco: Jossey-Bass.

West, M. A., & Anderson, N. R. (1996). Innovation in top management teams. *Journal of Applied Psychology, 81,* 680-693.

West, M., Lawthom, R., Patterson, M., & Staniforth, D. (1995). *Still far to go: The management of UK manufacturing.* Sheffield, UK: University of Sheffield.

Whybrow, A. C., & Parker, S. K. (1997, April). *Potholes, subsidence, and shifting horizons on the way to team working: The case of a steel making company.* Paper presented at the International Workshop on Teamworking, Nottingham, UK.

Wild, R. (1975). *Mass production work.* New York: John Wiley.

Wilkinson, A., Marchington, M., Goodman, J., & Ackers, P. (1992). Total quality management and employee involvement. *Human Resource Management Journal, 2,* 1-18.

Womack, J. P., Jones, D. T., & Roos, D. (1990). *The machine that changed the world.* New York: Rawson.

Wood, S. (1990). Tacit skills, the Japanese model and new technology. *Applied Psychology: An International Review, 39,* 169-190.

Wyatt, S., Fraser, J. A., & Stock, F. G. L. (1928). *The comparative effects of variety and uniformity in work* (Industrial Fatigue Research Board, Rep. No. 52). London: HMSO.

Wyatt, S., & Ogden, D. A. (1924). *On the extent and effects of variety and uniformity in repetitive work* (Industrial Fatigue Research Board, Rep. No. 26). London: HMSO.

Young, S. M. (1992). A framework for the successful adoption and performance of Japanese manufacturing practices in the United States. *Academy of Management Review, 17,* 677-700.

Author Index

157

Drasgow, F., 14
Dressel, P. L., 31
Drucker, P. F., 76
Dumler, M. P., 14
Dunham, R. B., 14
Dunphy, D., 22, 33
Dwyer, D. J., 48

Eisenstat, R. A., 124, 126
Emery, F. E., 9, 16, 17, 108, 110, 133
Endler, N. S., 34
Ephlin, D. F., 118
Ettlie, J. E., 76
Evans, M. G., 15

Fang, Y., 14
Farbey, B., 85, 86, 110
Farh, J., 27
Fay, D., 33
Fedor, D., 27
Feldman, D., 93
Fellman, 34
Ferris, G. R., 13, 14, 15, 16, 26
Fitter, M., 108
Fitzgerald, M. P., 15, 42
Fletcher, B. C., 48
Folger, R., 91
Ford, H., 1, 3, 4, 5, 77
Forssen-Nyberg, M., 128
Fox, M. L., 48
Fox, S., 92
Francis, C., 18
Francis, J., 31
Fraser, J. A., 6
Freeman, S. J., 90
Frese, M., 33, 34, 35, 37, 40, 41, 50, 51, 52
Fried, Y., 13, 14, 15, 16, 26
Frone, M. R., 87
Fullerton, H. N. Jr., 95

Galinsky, E., 35
Gallagher, D. G., 93
Ganster, D. C., 42, 48, 97
Garrahan, P., 67
Geary, J. F., 103
Geer, B., 35
George, J. F., 86
George, J. M., 33
Gilbert, M., 69
Gilbreth, F. B., 4, 53

Gladstein, D., 54
Glen, R., 18
Glick, W., 13, 26, 27, 28, 31, 33, 38, 42
Goiten, B., 37
Goldhar, J. D., 60, 76
Goodman, J., 62
Goodman, P. S., 17, 18, 24, 33, 34, 87, 88, 102, 106, 109, 132
Gormon, 21
Graham, I., 77
Grant, R. A., 75
Green, M. S., 97
Greenberg, E. R., 90
Grey, S. M., 105, 106, 108, 117
Griffin, R. W., 26, 27, 29
Griffith-Hughson, T. L., 17, 18, 24, 33, 34, 87, 88, 109, 132
Guest, R. H., 6, 8, 109
Gueutal, H. G., 31
Gunnarsson, E., 87
Guzzo, R. A., 16, 18, 40, 72

Hacker, W., 50
Hackman, J. R., 9, 11, 12, 13, 14, 17, 24, 32, 38, 54, 55, 97, 101, 102, 104, 105, 106, 108, 109, 114, 127, 134
Hakamaki, J., 128
Haldeman, J., 18
Halton, J., xiv
Hannover, B., 37
Harding, D. W., 7
Harvey, R. J., 14
Hatcher, L., 105
Hayes, R. H., 59, 75, 76
Hazelbaker, K. L., 92
Head, T. C., 26
Hedberg, B., 5
Hedlund, J., 90
Henne, D., 37
Herbst, P. G., 18
Herzberg, F., 8, 9, 10, 11, 20, 40, 43
Higgins, C. A., 75
Higgs, A. C., 54, 56, 83
Hilburger, T., 33
Hill, K. D., 114
Hill, S., 62
Hisrich, R. D., 33
Hochschild, A., 96
Hoffman, J., 5

Subject Index

About the Authors

Sharon Parker obtained her Bachelor of Science with honors in psychology at the University of Western Australia, Perth, Australia. She received her doctorate in occupational psychology from the Institute of Work Psychology, University of Sheffield, England, where she is now a Senior Research Fellow. Her research interests include work design, modern manufacturing initiatives, employee development, change processes, and equal opportunities. She has published articles in leading journals such as the *Academy of Management Journal,* the *Journal of Occupational Health Psychology,* and the *Journal of Applied Psychology,* and she has written several book chapters. She has considerable practical experience in working with organizations to help them redesign their work.

Toby Wall obtained his first degree and his doctorate in psychology from the University of Nottingham, England. He is Professor of Psychology at the University of Sheffield, where he is Director of the Institute of Work Psychology and the Economic and Social Research Council Centre for Organisation and Innovation. His main research interests have been in industrial and organizational psychology and have recently been focused on the effects of advanced manufacturing technology and shop floor work organization on work performance and strain. His research has appeared in the *Journal of Applied Psychology,* the *Academy of Management Journal,* and other leading publications, and he is the author of several books, including *The Human Side of Advanced Manufacturing Technology.*